Words of Our Nation

★

LIBRARY OF FREEDOM

Words of Our Nation

A READER
FOR AMERICANS

EDITED, WITH INTRODUCTIONS, BY
John Gabriel Hunt

GRAMERCY BOOKS
NEW YORK • AVENEL, NEW JERSEY

This 1993 edition is published by Gramercy Books,
distributed by Outlet Book Company, Inc.,
a Random House Company,
40 Engelhard Avenue,
Avenel, New Jersey 07001.

Random House
New York • Toronto • London • Sydney • Auckland

Designed by Helene Berinsky

Printed and bound in the United States of America

Library of Congress Cataloging-in-Publication Data
Words of our nation / edited by John Gabriel Hunt.
p. cm. — (Library of Freedom)
ISBN 0-517-09124-0
1. United States—History—Sources.   2. United States—Poetry.
I. Hunt, John Gabriel, 1952– .   II. Series.
E173.A525   1993   92-38740
973—dc20   CIP

8 7 6 5 4 3 2 1

CONTENTS

North and South

All Across the Land

The Social Fabric

Patriotism and Praise

INTRODUCTION

THE DRAMATIC MARCH of American history is celebrated in literature that ranges from the precious documents created by the Founding Fathers to verse of great emotion and patriotic fervor. *Words of Our Nation,* a collection of many of these pieces of the American mosaic, creates an exciting and inspirational panorama.

In each section of this book poetry, essays, letters, speeches, and documents reflect a significant theme or era of United States history. The introduction to each part places the various works—which are arranged chronologically—in their historical contexts.

"The Birth of a Nation" begins with early poems and essays that herald independence. The complete texts of the Declaration of Independence, the Constitution, and the Bill of Rights are included, as well as the major passages from the Articles of Confederation and Northwest Ordinance. Other poems, by Philip Freneau and Joaquin Miller, glorify specific events that occurred during the Revolutionary War.

"North and South" reveals the causes, heroism, and idealism of the Civil War. The beginnings of the conflict are reflected in the Missouri Compromise documents, in South Carolina's Declaration of Causes for its secession from the Union, and in Abraham Lincoln's impassioned House Divided speech. Poems written during the war proclaim both the agony and glory of such famous battles as Charleston, Gettysburg, and Shiloh. The assassination of Lincoln evoked many moving eulogies, including those by Walt Whitman, Paul Laurence Dunbar, and Vachel Lindsay.

"All Across the Land" is an exploration of the regions and cities of the United States, starting with documents by Presidents Jefferson and Monroe that deal with the nation's westward expansion. Poets, including John Greenleaf Whittier and Joaquin Miller, extolled the pioneering spirit, while Henry David Thoreau, Sidney Lanier, and John Muir painted marvelous prose pictures of rural New England, of cities of the South, and of the forests of the West.

"The Social Fabric" delineates the issues and concerns that have faced various segments of American society for two centuries: slavery, Native-American land, women's rights, labor issues, religious tolerance, and civil rights. Included are such important documents as the Tenth, Fourteenth, Nineteenth, and Twenty-fourth amendments to the Constitution, the Seneca Falls Women's Rights Convention Resolutions, President Franklin Roosevelt's National Recovery and Social Security acts, and presidential statements on Native-American policy.

In "Patriotism and Praise," early essays on the United States by J. Hector St. John de Crèvecoeur and Alexis de Tocqueville define a distinctly American spirit and character. Poets and writers, including Walt Whitman, Henry Ward Beecher, Francis Scott Key, and Joseph Rodman Drake sing the praises of democracy and the flag. In addition, there are evocations of the patriotic spirit, from poetry by Julia Ward Howe, John Greenleaf Whitter, Emma Lazarus, and others to the stirring 1941 inaugural address by President Franklin Roosevelt—and, of course, the Pledge of Allegiance to the Flag.

JOHN GABRIEL HUNT

New York
1993

★

PART ONE

The Birth of a Nation

A STRONG SPIRIT of patriotism prevailed during America's struggle for independence, and the events of the Revolution inspired poets and writers for years afterward. John Dickinson and Thomas Paine both wrote songs on the theme of liberty, and Timothy Dwight and Philip Freneau wrote poems in praise of the new nation and recorded the brave deeds of those who fought in the war. By the middle of the nineteenth century, many poets, including Henry Wadsworth Longfellow, Sidney Lanier, Joaquin Miller, and Oliver Wendell Holmes, were recalling, somewhat romantically, the days of the Revolution and the exploits of General Washington.

But the true record of the nation's birth is found in essays and documents written in the last quarter of the eighteenth century. Thomas Paine, for example, sparked the movement that established the independence of the American colonies with his pamphlet *Common Sense,* which was published anonymously in 1776. The poetic and inspiring Declaration of Independence was drafted by Thomas Jefferson, and in letters to his wife, Abigail, John Adams tells of the difficulties leading to its final adoption. In the Articles of Confederation (1781) and the Northwest Ordinance (1787) there can be seen the slow evolution of government and the struggle of disparate men and states to reach agreement, all of which finally culminated in the adoption of the Constitution and the Bill of Rights.

THE LIBERTY SONG

Come join hand in hand, brave Americans all,
And rouse your bold hearts at fair Liberty's call;
No tyrannous acts shall suppress your just claim,
Or stain with dishonor America's name.
In freedom we're born, and in freedom we'll live,
Our purses are ready,
Steady, friends, steady,
Not as slaves, but as freemen our money we'll give.

Our worthy forefathers—let's give them a cheer—
To climates unknown did courageously steer;
Thro' oceans to deserts for freedom they came,
And dying bequeath'd us their freedom and fame.

Their generous bosoms all dangers despis'd
So highly, so wisely, their birthrights they priz'd;
We'll keep what they gave, we will piously keep,
Nor frustrate their toils on the land and the deep.

The tree their own hands had to liberty rear'd
They live to behold growing strong and rever'd;
With transport then cried, "Now our wishes we gain,
For our children shall gather the fruits of our pain."

Swarms of placemen and pensioners soon will appear
Like locusts deforming the charms of the year;
Suns vainly will rise, showers vainly descend,
If we are to drudge for what others shall spend.

Then join hand in hand, brave Americans all,
By uniting we stand, by dividing we fall;
In so righteous a cause let us hope to succeed,
For heaven approves of each generous deed.

3

All ages shall speak with amaze and applause,
Of the courage we'll show in support of our laws;
To die we can bear—but to serve we disdain,
For shame is to freemen more dreadful than pain.

This bumper I crown for our sovereign's health,
And this for Britannia's glory and wealth;
That wealth and that glory immortal may be,
If she is but just, and if we are but free.

JOHN DICKINSON

A BALLAD OF THE BOSTON TEA PARTY

December 16, 1773

No! never such a draught was poured
    Since Hebe served with nectar
The bright Olympians and their Lord,
    Her overkind protector—
Since Father Noah squeezed the grape
    And took to such behaving
As would have shamed our grandsire ape
    Before the days of shaving—
No! ne'er was mingled such a draught
    In palace, hall, or arbor,
As freemen brewed and tyrants quaffed
    That night in Boston Harbor!
It kept King George so long awake
    His brain at last got addled,

It made the nerves of Britain shake,
　With sevenscore millions saddled;
Before that bitter cup was drained,
　Amid the roar of cannon,
The Western war-cloud's crimson stained
　The Thames, the Clyde, the Shannon;
Full many a six-foot grenadier
　The flattened grass had measured,
And, many a mother many a year
　Her tearful memories treasured;
Fast spread the tempest's darkening pall,
　The mighty realms were troubled,
The storm broke loose, but first of all
　The Boston teapot bubbled!

An evening party—only that,
　No formal invitation,
No gold-laced coat, no stiff cravat,
　No feast in contemplation,
No silk-robed dames, no fiddling band,
　No flowers, no songs, no dancing—
A tribe of red men, axe in hand—
　Behold the guests advancing!
How fast the stragglers join the throng,
　From stall and workshop gathered!
The lively barber skips along
　And leaves a chin half-lathered;
The smith has flung his hammer down—
　The horseshoe still is glowing;
The truant tapster at the Crown
　Has left a beer-cask flowing;
The cooper's boys have dropped the adze,
　And trot behind their master;
Up run the tarry shipyard lads—
　The crowd is hurrying faster—

Out from the millpond's purlieus gush
    The streams of white-faced millers,
And down their slippery alleys rush
    The lusty young Fort-Hillers;
The ropewalk lends its 'prentice crew—
    The Tories seize the omen:
"Ay, boys, you'll soon have work to do
    For England's rebel foemen,
'King Hancock,' Adams, and their gang,
    That fire the mob with treason—
When these we shoot and those we hang
    The town will come to reason."
On—on to where the ten-ships ride!
    And now their ranks are forming—
A rush, and up the Dartmouth's side
    The Mohawk band is swarming!
See the fierce natives! What a glimpse
    Of paint and fur and feather,
As all at once the full-grown imps
    Light on the deck together!
A scarf the pigtail's secret keeps,
    A blanket hides the breeches—
And out the cursed cargo leaps,
    And overhead it pitches!

O woman, at the evening board
    So gracious, sweet, and purring,
So happy while the tea is poured,
    So blest while spoons are stirring,
What martyr can compare with thee,
    The mother, wife, or daughter,
That night, instead of best Bohea,
    Condemned to milk and water!

Ah, little dreams the quiet dame
    Who plies with rock and spindle

The patient flax, how great a flame
   Yon little spark shall kindle!
The lurid morning shall reveal
   A fire no king can smother
Where British flint and Boston steel
   Have clashed against each other!
Old charters shrivel in its track,
   His Worship's bench has crumbled,
It climbs and clasps the Union Jack,
   Its blazoned pomp is humbled,
The flags go down on land and sea
   Like corn before the reapers;
So burned the fire that brewed the tea
   That Boston served her keepers!

The waves that wrought a century's wreck
   Have rolled o'er Whig and Tory;
The Mohawks on the Dartmouth's deck
   Still live in song and story;
The waters in the rebel bay
   Have kept the tea-leaf savor;
Our old North-Enders in their spray
   Still taste a Hyson flavor;
And Freedom's teacup still o'erflows
   With ever fresh libations,
To cheat of slumber all her foes
   And cheer the wakening nations!

OLIVER WENDELL HOLMES

PAUL REVERE'S RIDE

April 18, 1775

Listen, my children, and you shall hear
Of the midnight ride of Paul Revere,
On the eighteenth of April, in seventy-five;
Hardly a man is now alive
Who remembers that famous day and year.

He said to his friend, "If the British march
By land or sea from the town tonight,
Hang a lantern aloft in the belfry arch
Of the North Church tower as a signal light—
One, if by land, and two, if by sea;
And I on the opposite shore will be,
Ready to ride and spread the alarm
Through every Middlesex village and farm,
For the country folk to be up and to arm."

Then he said, "Good night!" and with muffled oar
Silently rowed to the Charlestown shore,
Just as the moon rose over the bay,
Where swinging wide at her moorings lay
The Somerset, British man-of-war;
A phantom ship, with each mast and spar
Across the moon like a prison bar,
And a huge black hulk, that was magnified
By its own reflection in the tide.

Meanwhile, his friend, through alley and street,
Wanders and watches with eager ears,
Till in the silence around him he hears
The muster of men at the barrack door,
The sound of arms, and the tramp of feet,

And the measured tread of the grenadiers,
Marching down to their boats on the shore.

Then he climbed the tower of the Old North Church,
By the wooden stairs, with stealthy tread,
To the belfry chamber overhead,
And startled the pigeons from their perch
On the somber rafters, that round him made
Masses and moving shapes of shade—
By the trembling ladder, steep and tall,
To the highest window in the wall,
Where he paused to listen and look down
A moment on the roofs of the town,
And the moonlight flowing over all.

Beneath, in the churchyard, lay the dead,
In their night-encampment on the hill,
Wrapped in silence so deep and still
That he could hear, like a sentinel's tread,
The watchful night wind, as it went
Creeping along from tent to tent,
And seeming to whisper, "All is well!"
A moment only he feels the spell
Of the place and the hour, and the secret dread
Of the lonely belfry and the dead;
For suddenly all his thoughts are bent
On a shadowy something far away,
Where the river widens to meet the bay—
A line of black that bends and floats
On the rising tide, like a bridge of boats.

Meanwhile, impatient to mount and ride,
Booted and spurred, with a heavy stride
On the opposite shore walked Paul Revere.
Now he patted his horse's side,
Now gazed at the landscape far and near,
Then, impetuous, stamped the earth,

And turned and tightened his saddle-girth;
But mostly he watched with eager search
The belfry tower of the Old North Church,
As it rose above the graves on the hill,
Lonely and spectral and somber and still.
And lo! as he looks, on the belfry's height
A glimmer, and then a gleam of light!
He springs to the saddle, the bridle he turns,
But lingers and gazes, till full on his sight
A second lamp in the belfry burns!

A hurry of hoofs in a village street,
A shape in the moonlight, a bulk in the dark,
And beneath, from the pebbles, in passing, a spark
Struck out by a steed flying fearless and fleet:
That was all! And yet, through the gloom and the light,
The fate of a nation was riding that night;
And the spark struck out by that steed, in his flight,
Kindled the land into flame with its heat.

He has left the village and mounted the steep,
And beneath him, tranquil and broad and deep,
Is the Mystic, meeting the ocean tides;
And under the alders, that skirt its edge,
Now soft on the sand, now loud on the ledge,
Is heard the tramp of his steed as he rides.

It was twelve by the village clock
When he crossed the bridge into Medford town.
He heard the crowing of the cock,
And the barking of the farmer's dog,
And felt the damp of the river fog,
That rises after the sun goes down.

It was one by the village clock,
When he galloped into Lexington.

He saw the gilded weathercock
Swim in the moonlight as he passed,
And the meeting-house windows, blank and bare,
Gaze at him with a spectral glare,
As if they already stood aghast
At the bloody work they would look upon.

It was two by the village clock,
When he came to the bridge in Concord town.
He heard the bleating of the flock,
And the twitter of birds among the trees,
And felt the breath of the morning breeze
Blowing over the meadows brown.
And one was safe and asleep in his bed
Who at the bridge would be first to fall,
Who that day would be lying dead,
Pierced by a British musket-ball.

You know the rest. In the books you have read,
How the British Regulars fired and fled—
How the farmers gave them ball for ball,
From behind each fence and farmyard wall,
Chasing the redcoats down the lane,
Then crossing the fields to emerge again
Under the trees at the turn of the road,
And only pausing to fire and load.

So through the night rode Paul Revere;
And so through the night went his cry of alarm
To every Middlesex village and farm—
A cry of defiance and not of fear,
A voice in the darkness, a knock at the door,
And a word that shall echo forevermore!
For, borne on the night wind of the past,
Through all our history, to the last,
In the hour of darkness and peril and need,

The people will waken and listen to hear
The hurrying hoofbeats of that steed,
And the midnight message of Paul Revere.

HENRY WADSWORTH LONGFELLOW

LEXINGTON

April 19, 1775

O'er Cambridge set the yeoman's mark:
Climb, patriot, through the April dark.
O lanthorn! kindle fast thy light,
Thou budding star in the April night,
For never a star more news hath told,
Or later flame in heaven shall hold.
Ay, lanthorn on the North Church tower,
When that thy church hath had her hour,
Still from the top of reverence high
Shalt thou illume Fame's ampler sky;
For, statured large o'er town and tree,
Time's tallest figure stands by thee,
And, dim as now thy wick may shine,
The Future lights his lamp at thine.

Now haste thee while the way is clear,
        Paul Revere!
Haste, Dawes! but haste thou not, O Sun!
        To Lexington.

Then Devens looked and saw the light:
He got him forth into the night,

And watched alone on the river shore,
And marked the British ferrying o'er.
John Parker! rub thine eyes and yawn,
But one o'clock and yet 'tis dawn!
Quick, rub thine eyes and draw thy hose:
The morning comes ere darkness goes.
Have forth and call the yeomen out,
For somewhere, somewhere close about
Full soon a thing must come to be
Thine honest eyes shall stare to see—
Full soon before thy patriot eyes
Freedom from out of a wound shall rise.

Then haste ye, Prescott and Revere!
Bring all the men of Lincoln here;
Let Chelmsford, Littleton, Carlisle,
Let Acton, Bedford, hither file—
Oh hither file, and plainly see
Out of a wound leap Liberty.
Say, Woodman April! all in green,
Say, Robin April! hast thou seen
In all thy travel round the earth
Ever a morn of calmer birth?
But Morning's eye alone serene
Can gaze across yon village green
To where the trooping British run
          Through Lexington.
Good men in fustian, stand ye still;
The men in red come o'er the hill.
Lay down your arms, damned rebels! cry
The men in red full haughtily.
But never a grounding gun is heard;
The men in fustian stand unstirred;
Dead calm, save maybe a wise bluebird
Puts in his little heavenly word.
O men in red! if ye but knew

The half as much as bluebirds do,
Now in this little tender calm
Each hand would out, and every palm
With patriot palm strike brotherhood's stroke
Or ere these lines of battle broke.

O men in red! if ye but knew
The least of the all that bluebirds do,
Now in this little godly calm
Yon voice might sing the future's psalm—
The psalm of love with the brotherly eyes
Who pardons and is very wise—
Yon voice that shouts, high-hoarse with ire,
　　Fire!
The redcoats fire, the homespuns fall:
The homespuns' anxious voices call,
Brother, art hurt? and *Where hit, John?*
And, *Wipe this blood,* and, *Men, come on,*
And, *Neighbor, do but lift my head,*
And, *Who is wounded? Who is dead?*
Seven are killed. My God! my God!
Seven lie dead on the village sod.
Two Harringtons, Parker, Hadley, Brown,
Monroe and Porter—these are down.
Nay, look! Stout Harrington not yet dead!
He crooks his elbow, lifts his head.
He lies at the step of his own house door;
He crawls and makes a path of gore.
The wife from the window hath seen, and rushed;
He hath reached the step, but the blood hath
　　gushed;
He hath crawled to the step of his own house door,
But his head hath dropped: he will crawl no more.
Clasp, wife, and kiss, and lift the head:
Harrington lies at his doorstep dead.

But, O ye six that round him lay
And bloodied up that April day!
As Harrington fell, ye likewise fell—
At the door of the house wherein ye dwell;
As Harrington came, ye likewise came
And died at the door of your house of fame.

SIDNEY LANIER

LIBERTY TREE

In a chariot of light from the regions of day,
The goddess of liberty came;
Ten thousand celestials directed the way,
And thither conducted the dame,
This fair budding branch, from the garden above,
Where millions with millions agree;
She bro't in her hand, as a pledge of her love,
The plant she call'd *Liberty Tree*.

This celestial exotic struck deep in the ground,
Like a native it flourish'd and bore;
The fame of its fruit, drew the nations around,
To seek out its peaceable shore.
Unmindful of names or distinction they came,
For freemen like brothers agree:
With one spirit endow'd, they one friendship pursued,
And their temple was *Liberty Tree*.

Beneath this fair branch, like the patriarchs of old,
Their bread, in contentment they eat;

Unwearied with trouble, of silver or gold,
Or the cares of the grand and the great.
With timber and tar, they old England supplied,
Supported her power on the seas;
Her battles they fought, without having a groat,
For the honor of *Liberty Tree.*

But hear, O ye swains ('tis a tale most profane),
How all the tyrannical powers,
King, commons, and lords, are uniting amain,
To cut down this guardian of ours;
From the East to the West, blow the trumpet to arms,
Thro' the land let the sound of it flee,
Let the far and the near—all unite with a cheer,
In defense of our *Liberty Tree.*

THOMAS PAINE

From John Adams to Abigail Adams: On General George Washington and the Congress

17 June 1775

I can now inform you, that the Congress have made choice of the modest and virtuous, the amiable, generous and brave George Washington, Esquire, to be General of the American army, and that he is to repair, as soon as possible, to the camp before Boston. This appointment will have a great effect in cementing and securing the union of these colonies. The continent is really in earnest, in defending the country. They have voted ten companies of riflemen to be sent from Pennsylvania, Maryland and Virginia, to join the army before Boston. These are an excellent species of light infantry. They use a peculiar kind of musket, called a rifle. It has circular or—grooves within the barrel, and carries a ball with great exactness to great distances. They are the most accurate marksmen in the world.

I begin to hope we shall not sit all summer. I hope the people of our province will treat the General with all that confidence and affection, that politeness and respect, which is due to one of the most important characters in the world. The liberties of America depend upon him, in a great degree. I have never been able to obtain from our province any regular and particular intelligence, since I left it. Kent, Swift, Tudor, Dr. Cooper, Dr. Winthrop and others wrote me often last fall; not a line from them this time.

I have found this Congress like the last. When we first came together, I found a strong jealousy of us from New England, and the Massachusetts in particular. Suspicions entertained of designs of independency; an American republic; presbyterian principles, and twenty other things. Our sentiments were heard in Congress with great caution, and seemed to make but little impression; but the longer we sat, the more clearly they saw the necessity of pushing vigorous measures. It has been so now. Every day we sit, the more we are convinced that the designs against us are hostile and sanguinary, and that nothing but fortitude, vigor, and perseverance can save us.

But America is a great unwieldy body. Its progress must be slow. It is like a large fleet sailing under convoy. The fleetest sailers must wait for the dullest and slowest. Like a coach and six, the swiftest horses must be slackened, and the slowest quickened, that all may keep an even pace.

It is long since I heard from you. I fear you have been kept in continual alarms. My duty and love to all. My dear children, come here and kiss me. We have appointed a continental fast. Millions will be upon their knees at once before their great Creator, imploring his forgiveness and blessing; his smiles on American councils and arms.

My duty to your uncle Quincy; your papa, mamma, and mine; my brothers and sisters, and yours. Adieu.

J. A.

FROM ABIGAIL ADAMS TO JOHN ADAMS: ON NEWS OF THE WAR

Boston, Sunday, 18 June 1775

Dearest Friend,

The day—perhaps the decisive day—is come, on which the fate of America depends. My bursting heart must find vent at my pen. I have just heard that our dear friend, Dr. Warren, is no more, but fell gloriously fighting for his country; saying, Better to die honorably in the field, than ignominiously hang upon the gallows. Great is our loss. He has distinguished himself in every engagement, by his courage and fortitude, by animating the soldiers, and leading them on by his own example. A particular account of these dreadful, but I hope glorious days, will be transmitted you, no doubt, in the exactest manner.

"The race is not to the swift, nor the battle to the strong; but the God of Israel is He that giveth strength and power unto his people. Trust in him at all times, ye people, pour out your hearts before him; God is a refuge for us." Charlestown is laid in ashes. The battle began upon our intrenchments upon Bunker's Hill, Saturday morning about three o'clock, and has not ceased yet, and it is now three o'clock Sabbath afternoon.

It is expected they will come out over the Neck tonight, and a dreadful battle must ensue. Almighty God, cover the heads of our countrymen, and be a shield to our dear friends! How many have fallen, we know not. The constant roar of the cannon is so distressing that we cannot eat, drink or sleep. May we be supported and sustained in the dreadful conflict. I shall tarry here till it is thought unsafe by my friends, and then I have secured myself a retreat at your brother's, who has kindly offered me part of his house. I cannot compose myself to write any further at present. I will add more as I hear further.

Tuesday afternoon

I have been so much agitated, that I have not been able to write since Sabbath day. When I say that ten thousand reports are passing, vague and uncertain as the wind, I believe I speak the truth. I am not able to give you any authentic account of last Saturday, but you will not be destitute of intelligence. Colonel Palmer has just sent me word that he has an opportunity of conveyance. Incorrect as this scrawl will be, it shall go. I ardently pray that you may be supported through the arduous task you have before you. I wish I could contradict the report of the Dr's death; but it is a lamentable truth, and the tears of the multitudes pay tribute to his memory; those favorite lines of Collins continually sound in my ears:

"How sleep the brave" etc.

I must close. . . . I have not pretended to be particular with regard to what I have heard because I know you will collect better intelligence. The spirits of the people are very good; the loss of Charlestown affects them no more than a drop in the bucket.

I am, most sincerely, yours,

PORTIA

FROM JOHN ADAMS TO ABIGAIL ADAMS: ON THE DECLARATION OF INDEPENDENCE

Philadelphia, 3 July, 1776

Had a Declaration of Independency been made seven months ago, it would have been attended with many great and glorious effects. We might, before this hour, have formed alliances with foreign states. We should have mastered Quebec, and been in possession of Canada. You will perhaps wonder how such a declaration would have influenced our affairs in Canada, but if I could write with freedom, I could easily convince you that it would, and explain to you the manner how. Many gentlemen in high stations, and of great influence, have been duped by the ministerial bubble of Commissioners to treat. And in real, sincere expectation of this event, which they so fondly wished, they have been slow and languid in promoting measures for the reduction of that province. Others there are in the Colonies who really wished that our enterprise in Canada would be defeated, that the Colonies might be brought into danger and distress between two fires, and be thus induced to submit. Others really wished to defeat the expedition to Canada, lest the conquest of it should elevate the minds of the people too much to hearken to those terms of reconciliation which, they believed, would be offered us. These jarring views, wishes, and designs occasioned an opposition to many salutary measures which were proposed for the support of that expedition, and caused obstructions, embarrassments, and studied delays, which have finally lost us the province.

All these causes, however, in conjunction would not have disappointed us, if it had not been for a misfortune which could not be foreseen, and perhaps could not have been prevented; I mean the prevalence of the small-pox among our troops. This fatal pestilence completed our destruction. It is a frown of Providence upon us, which we ought to lay to heart.

But, on the other hand, the delay of this Declaration to this time has many great advantages attending it. The hopes of reconciliation which were fondly entertained by multitudes of honest and well-meaning, though weak and mistaken people, have been gradually, and at last totally extinguished. Time has been given for the whole people maturely to consider the great question of independence, and to ripen their judgment, dissipate their fears, and allure their hopes, by discussing it in newspapers and pamphlets, by debating it in assemblies, conventions, committees of safety and inspection, in town and county meetings, as well as in private conversations, so that the whole people, in every colony of the thirteen, have now adopted it as their own act. This will cement the union, and avoid those heats, and perhaps convulsions, which might have been occasioned by such a Declaration six months ago.

But the day is past. The second day of July, 1776, will be the most memorable epocha in the history of America. I am apt to believe that it will be celebrated by succeeding generations as the great anniversary festival. It ought to be commemorated as the day of deliverance, by solemn acts of devotion to God Almighty. It ought to be solemnized with pomp and parade, with shows, games, sports, guns, bells, bonfires, and illuminations, from one end of this continent to the other, from this time forward forevermore.

You will think me transported with enthusiasm, but I am

not. I am well aware of the toil and blood and treasure that it will cost us to maintain this Declaration and support and defend these States. Yet, through all the gloom, I can see the rays of ravishing light and glory. I can see that the end is more than worth all the means. And that posterity will triumph in that day's transaction, even although we should rue it, which I trust in God we shall not.

J. A.

THE TIMES THAT TRY MEN'S SOULS

These are the times that try men's souls. The summer soldier and the sunshine patriot will, in this crisis, shrink from the service of their country; but he that stands it *now*, deserves the love and thanks of man and woman. Tyranny, like hell, is not easily conquered; yet we have this consolation with us, that the harder the conflict, the more glorious the triumph. What we obtain too cheap, we esteem too lightly: it is dearness only that gives everything its value. Heaven knows how to put a proper price upon its goods; and it would be strange indeed if so celestial an article as *freedom* should not be highly rated. Britain, with an army to enforce her tyranny, has declared that she has a right *not only to tax* but *"to bind us in all cases whatsoever,"* and if being *bound in that manner* is not slavery, then is there not such a thing as slavery upon earth. Even the expression is impious; for so unlimited a power can belong only to God.

Whether the independence of the continent was declared too soon, or delayed too long, I will not now enter into as an argument; my own simple opinion is, that had it been eight months earlier, it would have been much better. We did not make a proper use of last winter, neither could we, while we were in a dependent state. However, the fault, if it were one, was all our own; we have none to blame but ourselves. But no great deal is lost yet. All that Howe has been doing for this month past is rather a ravage than a conquest, which the spirit of the Jerseys, a year ago, would have quickly repulsed, and which time and a little resolution will soon recover.

I have as little superstition in me as any man living, but my secret opinion has ever been, and still is, that God Almighty will not give up a people to military destruction, or leave them unsupportedly to perish, who have so earnestly and so repeatedly sought to avoid the calamities of war, by every decent method which wisdom could invent. Neither have I so much of the infidel in me, as to suppose that He has relinquished the government of the world, and given us up to the care of devils; and as I do not, I cannot see on what grounds the king of Britain can look up to heaven for help against us: a common murderer, a highwayman, or a house-breaker, has as good a pretense as he.

THOMAS PAINE,
from *The Crisis*, 1776

On the Present State of
American Affairs

Volumes have been written on the subject of the struggle between England and America. Men of all ranks have embarked in the controversy, from different motives, and with various designs; but all have been ineffectual, and the period of debate is closed. Arms as the last resource decide the contest; the appeal was the choice of the king, and the continent has accepted the challenge. . . .

But Britain is the parent country, say some. Then the more shame upon her conduct. Even brutes do not devour their young, nor savages make war upon their families. Wherefore, the assertion, if true, turns to her reproach; but it happens not to be true, or only partly so, and the phrase *parent* or *mother country* hath been jesuitically adopted by the king and his parasites, with the low papistical design of gaining an unfair bias on the credulous weakness of our minds. Europe, and not England, is the parent country of America. This new world hath been the asylum for the persecuted lovers of civil and religious liberty from *every part* of Europe. Hither have they fled, not from the tender embraces of the mother, but from the cruelty of the monster; and it is so far true of England that the same tyranny which drove the first emigrants from home pursues their descendents still. . . .

I challenge the warmest advocate for reconciliation to show a single advantage that this continent can reap by being connected with Great Britain. I repeat the challenge; not a single advantage is derived. Our corn will fetch its price in any market in Europe, and our imported goods must be paid for, buy them where we will.

But the injuries and disadvantages which we sustain by that connection, are without number; and our duty to mankind at large, as well as to ourselves, instructs us to renounce the alliance: because any submission to, or dependence on, Great

Britain tends directly to involve this continent in European wars and quarrels and set us at variance with nations who would otherwise seek our friendship, and against whom we have neither anger nor complaint. As Europe is our market for trade, we ought to form no partial connection with any part of it. It is the true interest of America to steer clear of European contentions, which she can never do, while, by her dependence on Britain, she is made the make-weight in the scale of British politics.

Europe is too thickly planted with kingdoms to be long at peace, and whenever a war breaks out between England and any foreign power, the trade of America goes to ruin, *because of her connection with Britain.* The next war may not turn out like the last, and should it not, the advocates of reconciliation now will be wishing for separation then, because neutrality in that case would be a safer convoy than a man of war. Everything that is right or reasonable pleads for separation. The blood of the slain, the weeping voice of nature cries, *'Tis time to part.* Even the distance at which the Almighty hath placed England and America is a strong and natural proof that the authority of the one over the other, was never the design of heaven. The time likewise at which the continent was discovered, adds weight to the argument, and the manner in which it was peopled, increases the force of it. The Reformation was preceded by the discovery of America: as if the Almighty graciously meant to open a sanctuary to the persecuted in future years, when home should afford neither friendship nor safety.

The authority of Great Britain over this continent is a form of government which sooner or later must have an end: and a serious mind can draw no true pleasure by looking forward, under the painful and positive conviction that what he calls "the present constitution" is merely temporary. As parents, we can have no joy, knowing that this government is not sufficiently lasting to ensure anything which we may bequeath to posterity: and by a plain method of argument, as we are running the next generation into debt, we ought to do the work of it, otherwise we use them meanly and pitifully. In order to discover the line of our duty rightly, we should take our children in our hand, and fix our station a few years farther in life; that eminence will present a prospect which a few present fears and prejudices conceal from our sight.

Though I would carefully avoid giving unnecessary offense, yet I am inclined to believe that all those who espouse the doctrine of reconciliation may be included within the following descriptions.

Interested men, who are not to be trusted, weak men who *cannot* see, prejudiced men who will not see, and a certain set of moderate men who think better of the European world than it deserves; and this last class, by an ill-judged deliberation, will be the cause of more calamities to this continent than all the other three.

It is the good fortune of many to live distant from the scene of present sorrow; the evil is not sufficiently brought to their doors to make them feel the precariousness with which all American property is possessed. But let our imaginations transport us a few moments to Boston; that seat of wretchedness will teach us wisdom and instruct us forever to renounce a power in whom we can have no trust. The inhabitants of that unfortunate city who but a few months ago were in ease and affluence have now no other alternative than to stay and starve, or turn out to beg. Endangered by the fire of their friends if they continue within the city, and plundered by the soldiery if they leave it, in their present situation they are prisoners without the hope of redemption, and in a general attack for their relief they would be exposed to the fury of both armies.

Men of passive tempers look somewhat lightly over the offenses of Great Britain and, still hoping for the best, are apt to call out, *Come, come, we shall be friends again for all this.* But examine the passions and feelings of mankind; bring the doctrine of reconciliation to the touchstone of nature, and then tell me whether you can hereafter love, honor, and faithfully serve the power that hath carried fire and sword into your land? If you cannot do all these, then are you only deceiving yourselves, and by your delay bringing ruin upon posterity. Your future connection with Britain, whom you can neither love nor honor, will be forced and unnatural and, being formed only on the plan of present convenience, will in a little time fall into a relapse more wretched than the first. But if you say, you can still pass the violations over, then I ask, hath your house been burnt? Hath your property been destroyed before your face? Are your wife and children destitute of a bed to lie on, or bread to live on? Have you lost a parent or a child by their hands, and yourself the ruined and wretched survivor? If you have not, then you are not a judge of those who have. But if you have, and can still shake hands with the murderers, then are you unworthy of the name of husband, father, friend, or lover, and whatever may be your rank or title in life, you have the heart of a coward and the spirit of a sycophant.

This is not inflaming or exaggerating matters but trying them by those feelings and affections which nature justifies, and without which we should be incapable of discharging the social duties of life or enjoying the felicities of it. I mean not to exhibit horror for the purpose of provoking revenge, but to awaken us from fatal and unmanly slumbers, that we may pursue determinedly some fixed object. 'Tis not in the power of Britain or of Europe to conquer America, if she doth not conquer herself by delay and timidity. The present winter is worth an age if rightly employed, but if lost or neglected the whole continent will partake of the misfortune; and there is no punishment which that man doth not deserve, be he who or what, or where he will, that may be the means of sacrificing a season so precious and useful.

'Tis repugnant to reason, to the universal order of things, to all the examples of former ages, to suppose that this continent can long remain subject to any external power. The most sanguine in Britain doth not think so. The utmost stretch of human wisdom cannot, at this time, compass a plan, short of separation, which can promise the continent even a year's security. Reconciliation is *now* a fallacious dream. Nature hath deserted the connection, and art cannot supply her place. For, as Milton wisely expresses, "never can true reconcilement grow where wounds of deadly hate have pierced so deep."

Every quiet method for peace hath proved ineffectual. Our prayers have been rejected with disdain; and only tended to convince us that nothing flatters vanity or confirms obstinacy in kings more than repeated petitioning—and nothing hath contributed more than that very measure to make the kings of Europe absolute. Witness Denmark and Sweden. Wherefore, since nothing but blows will do, for God's sake let us come to a final separation, and not leave the next generation to be cutting throats under the violated unmeaning names of parent and child.

THOMAS PAINE,
from *Common Sense*, 1776

THE DECLARATION OF INDEPENDENCE

July 4, 1776

When in the course of human events, it becomes necessary for one people to dissolve the political bands which have connected them with another, and to assume among the powers of the earth the separate and equal station to which the laws of nature and of nature's God entitle them, a decent respect to the opinions of mankind requires that they should declare the causes which impel them to the separation.

We hold these truths to be self-evident: that all men are created equal, that they are endowed by their Creator with certain unalienable rights, that among these are life, liberty, and the pursuit of happiness. That to secure these rights, governments are instituted among men, deriving their just powers from the consent of the governed; that whenever any form of government becomes destructive of these ends, it is the right of the people to alter or to abolish it, and to institute new government, laying its foundation on such principles and organizing its powers in such form, as to them shall seem most likely to effect their safety and happiness.

Prudence, indeed, will dictate that governments long established should not be changed for light and transient causes; and accordingly all experience hath shown, that mankind are more disposed to suffer, while evils are sufferable, than to right themselves by abolishing the forms to which they are accustomed. But when a long train of abuses and usurpations, pursuing invariably the same object, evinces a design to reduce them under absolute despotism, it is their right, it is their duty, to throw off such government, and to provide new guards for their future security. Such has been the patient sufferance of these colonies; and such is now the necessity which constrains them to alter their former systems of government.

The history of the present king of Great Britain is a history of repeated injuries and usurpations, all having in direct object the establishment of an absolute tyranny over these states. To prove this, let facts be submitted to a candid world.

He has refused his assent to laws, the most wholesome and necessary for the public good.

He has forbidden his governors to pass laws of immediate and pressing importance, unless suspended in their operation till his assent should be obtained; and when so suspended, he has utterly neglected to attend to them.

He has refused to pass other laws for the accommodation of large districts of people, unless those people would relinquish the right of representation in the legislature, a right inestimable to them and formidable to tyrants only.

He has called together legislative bodies at places unusual, uncomfortable, and distant from the depository of their public records, for the sole purpose of fatiguing them into compliance with his measures.

He has dissolved representative houses repeatedly for opposing with manly firmness his invasions on the rights of the people.

He has refused for a long time, after such dissolutions, to cause others to be elected; whereby the legislative powers, incapable of annihilation, have returned to the people at large for their exercise; the state remaining in the meantime exposed to all the dangers of invasion from without, and convulsions within.

He has endeavored to prevent the population of these states; for that purpose obstructing the laws for naturalization of foreigners; refusing to pass others to encourage their migration hither, and raising the conditions of new appropriations of lands.

He has obstructed the administration of justice, by refusing his assent to laws for establishing judiciary powers.

He has made judges dependent on his will alone, for the tenure of their offices, and the amount and payment of their salaries.

He has erected a multitude of new offices, and sent hither swarms of officers to harass our people and eat out their substance.

He has kept among us, in times of peace, standing armies without the consent of our legislature.

He has affected to render the military independent of and superior to the civil power.

He has combined with others to subject us to a jurisdiction foreign to our constitution, and unacknowledged by our laws; giving his assent to their acts of pretended legislation:

For quartering large bodies of armed troops among us;

For protecting them, by a mock trial, from punishment for any murders which they should commit on the inhabitants of these states;

For cutting off our trade with all parts of the world;

For imposing taxes on us without our consent;

For depriving us, in many cases, of the benefits of trial by jury;

For transporting us beyond seas to be tried for pretended offenses;

For abolishing the free system of English laws in a neighboring province, establishing therein an arbitrary government, and enlarging its boundaries so as to render it at once an example and fit instrument for introducing the same absolute rule into these colonies;

For taking away our charters, abolishing our most valuable laws, and altering fundamentally the forms of our governments;

For suspending our own legislatures, and declaring themselves invested with power to legislate for us in all cases whatsoever.

He has abdicated government here by declaring us out of his protection and waging war against us.

He has plundered our seas, ravaged our coasts, burnt our towns, and destroyed the lives of our people.

He is at this time transporting large armies of foreign mercenaries to complete the works of death, desolation, and tyranny, already begun with circumstances of cruelty and perfidy scarcely paralleled in the most barbarous ages, and totally unworthy the head of a civilized nation.

He has constrained our fellow citizens taken captive on the high seas to bear arms against their country, to become the executioners of their friends and brethren, or to fall themselves by their hands.

He has excited domestic insurrections amongst us, and has endeavored to bring on the inhabitants of our frontiers, the merciless Indian savages, whose known rule of warfare is an undistinguished destruction of all ages, sexes, and conditions.

In every stage of these oppressions we have petitioned for redress in the most humble terms; our repeated petitions have been answered only by repeated injury. A prince, whose character is thus marked by every act which may define a tyrant, is unfit to be the ruler of a free people.

Nor have we been wanting in attention to our British brethren. We have warned them from time to time of attempts by their legislature to extend an unwarrantable jurisdiction over us. We have reminded them of the circumstances of our emigration and settlement here. We have appealed to their native justice and magnanimity, and we have conjured them by the ties of our common kindred to disavow these usurpations, which would inevitably interrupt our connections and correspondence. They too have been deaf to the voice of justice and of consanguinity. We must, therefore, acquiesce in the necessity which denounces our separation, and hold them, as we hold the rest of mankind, enemies in war, in peace, friends.

We, therefore, the representatives of the United States of America, in general congress assembled, appealing to the Supreme Judge of the world for the rectitude of our intentions, do, in the name and by authority of the good people of these colonies, solemnly publish and declare, that these united colonies are, and of right ought to be, free and independent states; that they are absolved from all allegiance to the British crown, and that all political connection between them and the state of Great Britain is, and ought to be, totally dissolved; and that as free and independent states they have full power to levy war, conclude peace, contract alliances, establish commerce, and to do all other acts and things which independent states may of right do. And for the support of this declaration, with a firm reliance on the protection of Divine Providence, we mutually pledge to each other our lives, our fortunes, and our sacred honor.

WASHINGTON BY THE DELAWARE

December 25, 1776

The snow was red with patriot blood,
The proud foe tracked the blood-red snow.
The flying patriots crossed the flood
A tattered, shattered band of woe.
Forlorn each barefoot hero stood,
With bare head bended low.

"Let us cross back! Death waits us here:
Recross or die!" the chieftain said.
A famished soldier dropped a tear—
A tear that froze as it was shed:
For oh, his starving babes were dear—
They had but this for bread!

A captain spake: "It cannot be!
These bleeding men, why, what could they?

'Twould be as snowflakes in the sea!"
The worn chief did not heed or say.
He set his firm lips silently,
Then turned aside to pray.

And as he kneeled and prayed to God,
God's finger spun the stars in space;
He spread his banner blue and broad,
He dashed the dead sun's stripes in place,
Till war walked heaven fire shod
And lit the chieftain's face:

Till every soldier's heart was stirred,
Till every sword shook in its sheath—
"Up! up! Face back. But not one word!"
God's flag above; the ice beneath—
They crossed so still, they only heard
The icebergs grind their teeth!

Ho! Hessians, hirelings at meat
While praying patriots hunger so!
Then, bang! Boom! Bang! Death and defeat!
And blood? Ay, blood upon the snow!
Yet not the blood of patriot feet,
But heart's blood of the foe!

O ye who hunger and despair!
O ye who perish for the sun,
Look up and dare, for God is there;
And man can do what man has done!
Think, think of darkling Delaware!
Think, think of Washington!

JOAQUIN MILLER

COLUMBIA

Columbia, Columbia, to glory arise,
The queen of the world, and child of the skies!
Thy genius commands thee; with rapture behold,
While ages on ages thy splendors unfold.
Thy reign is the last, and the noblest of time,
Most fruitful thy soil, most inviting thy clime;
Let the crimes of the East ne'er encrimson thy name,
Be freedom, and science, and virtue, thy fame.
To conquest, and slaughter, let Europe aspire:
Whelm nations in blood, and wrap cities in fire:
Thy heroes the rights of mankind shall defend,
And triumph pursue them, and glory attend.
A world is thy realm: for a world be thy laws,
Enlarg'd as thine empire, and just as thy cause;
On freedom's broad basis, that empire shall rise,
Extend with the main, and dissolve with the skies.
Fair Science her gates to thy sons shall unbar,
And the East see thy morn hide the beams of her star.
New bards, and new sages, unrival'd shall soar
To fame unextinguish'd when time is no more;
To thee, the last refuge of virtue design'd,
Shall fly from all nations the best of mankind;
Here, grateful to heaven, with transport shall bring
Their incense, more fragrant than odors of spring.
Nor less shall thy fair ones to glory ascend,
And genius and beauty in harmony blend;
The graces of form shall awake pure desire,
And the charms of the soul ever cherish the fire;
Their sweetness unmingled, their manners refin'd,
And Virtue's bright image, instamp'd on the mind,
With peace and soft rapture shall teach life to glow,
And light up a smile in the aspect of woe.

Thy fleets to all regions thy pow'r shall display,
The nations admire, and the oceans obey;
Each shore to thy glory its tribute unfold,
And the East and the South yield their spices and gold.

As the day-spring unbounded, thy splendor shall flow,
And earth's little kingdoms before thee shall bow;
While the ensigns of union, in triumph unfurl'd,
Hush the tumult of war, and give peace to the world.
   Thus, as down a lone valley, with cedars o'erspread,
From war's dread confusion I pensively stray'd—
The gloom from the face of fair heav'n retir'd;
The winds ceas'd to murmur; the thunders expir'd;
Perfumes, as of Eden, flow'd sweetly along,
And a voice, as of angels, enchantingly sung:
"Columbia, Columbia, to glory arise,
The queen of the world and the child of the skies."

TIMOTHY DWIGHT

THE ARTICLES OF CONFEDERATION

March 1, 1781

To all to whom these presents shall come, we the undersigned delegates of the states affixed to our names send greeting. *Whereas*, The delegates of the United States of America in Congress assembled did on the fifteenth day of November in the year of Our Lord one thousand seven hundred and seventy seven, and in the second year of the independence of America, agree to certain articles of confederation and perpetual union between the states of New Hampshire, Massachusetts Bay, Rhode Island and Providence Plantations, Connecticut, New York, New Jersey, Pennsylvania, Delaware, Maryland, Virginia, North Carolina, South Carolina, and Georgia in the words following, viz.,

"Articles of Confederation and perpetual union between the states of New Hampshire, Massachusetts Bay, Rhode Island and Providence Plantations, Connecticut, New York, New Jersey, Pennsylvania, Delaware, Maryland, Virginia, North Carolina, South Carolina, and Georgia."

ARTICLE I

The style of this confederacy shall be "The United States of America."

ARTICLE II

Each state retains its sovereignty, freedom, and independence, and every power, jurisdiction, and right, which is not by this confederation expressly delegated to the United States, in Congress assembled.

ARTICLE III

The said states hereby severally enter into a firm league of friendship with each other for their common defense, the security of their liberties, and their mutual and general welfare, binding themselves to assist each other against all force offered to, or attacks made upon them, or any of them, on account of religion, sovereignty, trade, or any other pretense whatever.

ARTICLE IV

The better to secure and perpetuate mutual friendship and intercourse among the people of the different states in this union, the free inhabitants of each of these states—paupers, vagabonds, and fugitives from justice excepted—shall be entitled to all privileges and immunities of free citizens in the several states; and the people of each state shall have free ingress and regress to and from any other state, and shall enjoy therein all the privileges of trade and commerce, subject to the same duties, impositions, and restrictions as the inhabitants thereof respectively, provided that such restrictions shall not extend so far as to prevent the removal of property imported into any state, to any other state of which the owner is an inhabitant; provided also that no imposition, duties, or restriction shall be laid by any state on the property of the United States, or either of them.

If any person guilty of, or charged with treason, felony, or other high misdemeanor in any state shall flee from justice, and be found in any of the United States, he shall upon demand of the governor or executive power of the state from which he fled be delivered up and removed to the state having jurisdiction of his offense.

Full faith and credit shall be given in each of these states to the records, acts, and judicial proceedings of the courts and magistrates of every other state.

ARTICLE V

For the more convenient management of the general interests of the United States, delegates shall be annually appointed in such manner as the legislature of each state shall direct, to meet in Congress on the first Monday in November, in every year, with a power reserved to each state to recall its delegates, or any of them, at any time within the year, and to send others in their stead for the remainder of the year.

No state shall be represented in Congress by less than two, nor by more than seven members; and no person shall be capable of being a delegate for more than three years in any term of six years; nor shall any person, being a delegate, be capable of holding any office under the United States for which he, or another for his benefit, receives any salary, fees, or emolument of any kind.

Each state shall maintain its own delegates in a meeting of the states, and while they act as members of the committee of the states.

In determining questions in the United States in Congress assembled, each state shall have one vote.

Freedom of speech and debate in Congress shall not be impeached or questioned in any court, or place out of Congress, and the members of Congress shall be protected in their persons from arrests and imprisonments during the time of their going to and from, and attendance on Congress, except for treason, felony, or breach of the peace.

ARTICLE VI

No state without the consent of the United States in Congress assembled shall send any embassy to, or receive any embassy from, or enter into any conference, agreement, or alliance or treaty with any king, prince, or state; nor shall any person holding any office of profit or trust under the United States, or any of them, accept of any present, emolument, office, or title of any kind whatever from any king, prince, or foreign state; nor shall the United States in Congress assembled, or any of them, grant any title of nobility.

No two or more states shall enter into any treaty, confederation, or alliance whatever between them without the consent of the United States in Congress assembled, specifying accurately the purposes for which the same is to be entered into, and how long it shall continue.

No state shall lay any imposts or duties which may interfere with any stipulations in treaties entered into by the United States in Congress assembled, with any king, prince, or state, in pursuance of any treaties already proposed by Congress to the courts of France and Spain.

No vessels of war shall be kept up in time of peace by any state, except such number only as shall be deemed necessary by the United States in Congress assembled, for the defense of such state, or its trade; nor shall any body of forces be kept up by any state in time of peace, except such number only as in the judgment of the United States, in Congress assembled, shall be deemed requisite to garrison the forts necessary for the defense of such state; but every state shall always keep up a well-regulated and disciplined militia, sufficiently armed and accoutered, and shall provide and constantly have ready for use, in public stores, a due number of field pieces and tents, and a proper quantity of arms, ammunition, and camp equipage.

No state shall engage in any war without the consent of the United States in Congress assembled, unless such state be actually invaded by enemies, or shall have received certain advice of a resolution being formed by some nation of Indians to invade such state, and the danger is so imminent as not to admit of a delay till the United States in Congress assembled can be consulted. . . .

ARTICLE VII

When land forces are raised by any state for the common defense, all officers of or under the rank of colonel shall be appointed by the legislature of each state respectively by whom such forces shall be raised, or in such manner as such state shall direct, and all vacancies shall be filled up by the state which first made the appointment.

ARTICLE VIII

All charges of war, and all other expenses that shall be incurred for the common defense or general welfare, and allowed by the United States in Congress assembled, shall be defrayed out of a common treasury, which shall be supplied by the several states in proportion to the value of all land within each state, granted to or surveyed for any person, as such land and the buildings and improvements thereon shall be estimated according to such mode as the United States in Congress assembled shall from time to time direct and appoint. . . .

ARTICLE IX

The United States in Congress assembled shall have the sole and exclusive right and power of determining on peace and war, except in the cases mentioned in the sixth article—of sending and receiving ambassadors—entering into treaties and alliances, provided that no treaty of commerce shall be made whereby the legislative power of the respective states shall be restrained from imposing such imposts and duties on foreigners, as their own people are subjected to, or from prohibiting the exportation or importation of any species of goods or commodities whatsoever—of establishing rules for deciding in all cases, what captures on land or water shall be legal, and in what manner prizes taken by land or naval forces in the service of the United States shall be divided or appropriated—of granting letters of marque and reprisal in times of peace—appointing courts for the trial of piracies and felonies committed on the high seas and establishing courts for receiving and determining finally appeals in all cases of captures, provided that no member of Congress shall be appointed a judge of any of the said courts.

The United States in Congress assembled shall also be the last resort on appeal in all disputes and differences now subsisting or that hereafter may arise between two or more states concerning boundary, jurisdiction, or any other cause whatever. . . .

All controversies concerning the private right of soil claimed under different grants of two or more states, whose jurisdiction as they may respect such lands, and the states which passed such grants are adjusted, the said grants or either of them being at the same time claimed to have originated antecedent to such settlement of jurisdiction, shall on the petition of either party to the Congress of the United States be finally determined as near as may be in the same manner as is before prescribed for deciding disputes respecting territorial jurisdiction between different states.

The United States in Congress assembled shall also have the sole and exclusive right and power of regulating the alloy and value of coin struck by their own authority, or by that of the respective states—fixing the standard of weights and measures throughout the United States—regulating the trade and managing all affairs with the Indians, not members of any of the states, provided that the legislative right of any state within its own limits be not infringed or violated—establishing and regulating post offices from one state to another throughout all the United States, and exacting such postage on the papers passing through the same as may be requisite to defray the expenses of the said office—appointing all officers of the land forces in the service of the United States, excepting regimental officers—appointing all the officers of the naval forces, and commissioning all officers whatever in the service of the United States—making rules for the government and regulation of the said land and naval forces, and directing their operations.

The United States in Congress assembled shall have authority to appoint a committee to sit in the recess of Congress, to be denominated a Committee of the States, and to consist of one delegate from each state; and to appoint such other committees and civil officers as may be necessary for managing the general affairs of the United States under their direction—to appoint one of their number to preside, provided that no person be allowed to serve in the office of president more than one year in any term of three years; to ascertain the necessary sums of money to be raised for the service of the United States, and to appropriate and apply the same for defraying the public expenses—to borrow money or emit bills on the credit of the United States, transmitting every half-year to the respective states an account of the sums of money so borrowed or emitted—to build and equip a navy—to agree upon the number of land forces, and to make requisitions from each state for its quota in proportion to the number of white inhabitants in each state; which requisition shall be binding, and thereupon the legislature of each state shall appoint the regimental officers, raise the men, and clothe, arm, and equip them in a soldierlike manner at the expense of the United States, and the officers and men so clothed, armed, and equipped shall march to the place appointed, and within the time agreed on by the United States in Congress assembled. . . .

The United States in Congress assembled shall never engage in a war, nor grant letters of marque and reprisal in time of peace, nor enter into any treaties or alliances, nor coin money, nor regulate the value thereof, nor ascertain the sums and expenses necessary for the defense and welfare of the United States, or any of them, nor emit bills, nor borrow money on the credit of the United States, nor appropriate money, nor agree upon the number of vessels of war to be built or purchased, nor the number of land or sea forces to be raised, nor appoint a commander in chief of the army or navy, unless nine states assent to the same: nor shall a question on any other point, except for adjourning from day to day, be determined unless by the votes of a majority of the United States in Congress assembled.

The Congress of the United States shall have power to adjourn to any time within the year, and to any place within the United States, so that no period of adjournment be for a longer duration than the space of six months, and shall publish the journal of their proceedings monthly, except such parts thereof relating to treaties, alliances, or military operations, as in their judgment require secrecy; and the yeas and nays of the delegates of each state on any question shall be entered on the journal when it is desired by any delegate; and the delegates of a state, or any of them, at his or their request shall be furnished with a transcript of the said journal, except such parts as are above excepted, to lay before the legislatures of the several states.

ARTICLE X

The Committee of the States, or any nine of them, shall be authorized to execute, in the recess of Congress, such of the powers of Congress as the United States in Congress assembled, by the consent of nine states, shall from time to time think expedient to vest them with; provided that no power be delegated to the said committee for the exercise of which, by the Articles of Confederation, the voice of nine states in the Congress of the United States assembled is requisite.

ARTICLE XI

Canada acceding to this confederation, and joining in the measures of the United States, shall be admitted into, and entitled to all the advantages of this union: but no other colony shall be admitted into the same unless such admission be agreed to by nine states.

ARTICLE XII

All bills of credit emitted, monies borrowed, and debts contracted by, or under the authority of Congress, before the assembling of the United States, in pursuance of the present confederation, shall be deemed and considered as a charge against the United States, for payment and satisfaction whereof the said United States and the public faith are hereby solemnly pledged.

ARTICLE XIII

Every state shall abide by the determinations of the United States in Congress assembled on all questions which, by this confederation, are submitted to them. And the articles of this confederation shall be inviolably observed by every state, and the union shall be perpetual; nor shall any alteration at any time hereafter be made in any of them, unless such alteration be agreed to in a Congress of the United States, and be afterward confirmed by the legislatures of every state.

And Whereas, It hath pleased the Great Governor of the World to incline the hearts of the legislatures we respectively represent in Congress to approve of, and to authorize us to ratify, the said Articles of Confederation and perpetual union: *Know Ye,* That we the undersigned delegates, by virtue of the power and authority to us given for that purpose, do by these presents, in the name and in behalf of our respective constitu ents, fully and entirely ratify and confirm each and every of the said Articles of Confederation and perpetual union, and all and singular the matters and things therein contained: and we do further solemnly plight and engage the faith of our respective constituents, that they shall abide by the determinations of the United States in Congress assembled on all questions which, by the said confederation, are submitted to them. And that the articles thereof shall be inviolably observed by the states we respectively represent, and that the union shall be perpetual. In witness whereof we have hereunto set our hands in Congress.

Done at Philadelphia in the state of Pennsylvania the ninth day of July in the year of Our Lord one thousand seven hundred and seventy-eight, and in the third year of the independence of America.

TO THE MEMORY OF THE BRAVE AMERICANS

Under General Greene, in South Carolina,
Who Fell in the Action of September 8, 1781

At Eutaw Springs the valiant died;
   Their limbs with dust are covered o'er—
Weep on, ye springs, your tearful tide;
   How many heroes are no more!

If in this wreck of ruin, they
   Can yet be thought to claim a tear,
O smite your gentle breast, and say
   The friends of freedom slumber here!

Thou, who shalt trace this bloody plain,
   If goodness rules thy generous breast,
Sigh for the wasted rural reign;
   Sigh for the shepherds, sunk to rest!

Stranger, their humble graves adorn;
   You too may fall, and ask a tear;
'Tis not the beauty of the morn
   That proves the evening shall be clear.

They saw their injured country's woe;
   The flaming town, the wasted field;
Then rushed to meet the insulting foe;
   They took the spear—but left the shield.

Led by thy conquering genius, Greene,
   The Britons they compelled to fly;
None distant viewed the fatal plain,
   None grieved, in such a cause to die—

But, like the Parthian, famed of old,
  Who, flying, still their arrows threw,
These routed Britons, full as bold,
  Retreated, and retreating slew.

Now rest in peace, our patriot band;
  Though far from nature's limits thrown,
We trust they find a happier land,
  A brighter sunshine of their own.

PHILIP FRENEAU

THE NORTHWEST ORDINANCE

*An Ordinance for the Government of
the Territory of the United States
Northwest of the River Ohio, July 13, 1787*

Be it ordained by the United States in Congress assembled, That the said territory, for the purposes of temporary government, be one district, subject, however, to be divided into two districts as future circumstances may, in the opinion of Congress, make it expedient.

Be it ordained by the authority aforesaid, That the estates, both of resident and nonresident proprietors in the said territory, dying intestate, shall descend to, and be distributed among, their children and the descendants of a deceased child in equal parts; the descendants of a deceased child or grandchild to take the share of their deceased parent in equal parts among them; and where there shall be no children or descendants, then in equal parts to the next of kin in equal degree; and among collaterals, the children of a deceased brother or sister of the intestate shall have, in equal parts among them, their deceased parents' share; and there shall in no case be a distinction between kindred of the whole and half-blood; saving, in all cases, to the widow of the intestate her third part of the real estate for life, and one-third part of the personal estate; and this law relative to descents and dower shall remain in full force until altered by the legislature of the district.

And until the governor and judges shall adopt laws as hereinafter mentioned, estates in the said territory may be devised or bequeathed by wills in writing, signed and sealed by him or her in whom the estate may be (being of full age) and attested by three witnesses; and real estates may be conveyed by lease and release, or bargain and sale, signed, sealed, and delivered by the person, being of full age, in whom the estate may be, and attested by two witnesses. . . .

Be it ordained by the authority aforesaid, That there shall be appointed, from time to time, by Congress, a governor, whose commission shall continue in force for the term of three years, unless sooner revoked by Congress; he shall reside in the district, and have a freehold estate therein, in one thousand acres of land while in the exercise of his office.

There shall be appointed from time to time, by Congress, a secretary, whose commission shall continue in force for four years unless sooner revoked; he shall reside in the district, and have a freehold estate therein, in five hundred acres of land while in the exercise of his office. It shall be his duty to keep and preserve the acts and laws passed by the legislature, and the public records of the district, and the proceedings of the governor in his executive department, and transmit authentic copies of such acts and proceedings every six months to the secretary of Congress. There shall also be appointed a court, to consist of three judges, any two of whom to form a court, who shall have a common law jurisdiction, and reside in the district, and have each therein a freehold estate in five hundred acres of land while in the exercise of their offices; and their commissions shall continue in force during good behavior.

The governor and judges, or a majority of them, shall adopt and publish in the district such laws of the original states, criminal and civil, as may be necessary and best suited to the circumstances of the district, and report them to Congress from time to time; which laws shall be in force in the district until the organization of the general assembly therein, unless disapproved of by Congress; but afterward the legislature shall have authority to alter them as they shall think fit.

The governor, for the time being, shall be commander in chief of the militia, appoint and commission all officers in the same below the rank of general officers; all general officers shall be appointed and commissioned by Congress.

Previous to the organization of the general assembly, the governor shall appoint such magistrates and other civil officers in each county or township as he shall find necessary for the preservation of the peace and good order in the same. After the general assembly shall be organized, the powers and duties of the magistrates and other civil officers shall be regulated and defined by the said assembly; but all magistrates and other civil officers not herein otherwise directed shall, during the continuance of this temporary government, be appointed by the governor.

For the prevention of crimes and injuries, the laws to be adopted or made shall have force in all parts of the district, and for the execution of process, criminal and civil, the governor shall make proper divisions thereof; and he shall proceed from time to time, as circumstances may require, to lay out the parts of the district in which the Indian titles shall have been extinguished, into counties and townships, subject, however, to such alterations as may thereafter be made by the legislature.

So soon as there shall be five thousand free male inhabitants of full age in the district, upon giving proof thereof to the governor, they shall receive authority, with time and place, to elect representatives from their counties or townships to represent them in the general assembly:

Provided, That, for every five hundred free male inhabitants, there shall be one representative, and so on, progressively, with the number of free male inhabitants, shall the right of representation increase, until the number of representatives shall amount to twenty-five; after which, the number and proportion of representatives shall be regulated by the legislature:

Provided, That no person be eligible or qualified to act as a representative unless he shall have been a citizen of one of the United States three years, and be a resident in the district, or unless he shall have resided in the district three years; and, in either case, shall likewise hold in his own right, in fee simple, two hundred acres of land within the same:

Provided, also, That a freehold in fifty acres of land in the district, having been a citizen of one of the states, and being resident in the district, or the like freehold and two years' residence in the district, shall be necessary to qualify a man as an elector of a representative.

The representatives thus elected shall serve for the term of two years; and in case of the death of a representative, or removal from office, the governor shall issue a writ to the county or township for which he was a member, to elect another in his stead to serve for the residue of the term.

The general assembly or legislature shall consist of the governor, legislative council, and a house of representatives. The legislative council shall consist of five members, to continue in office five years unless sooner removed by Congress; any three of whom to be a quorum: and the members of the council shall be nominated and appointed in the following manner, to wit:

As soon as representatives shall be elected, the governor shall appoint a time and place for them to meet together; and, when met, they shall nominate ten persons, residents in the district and each possessed of a freehold in five hundred acres of land, and return their names to Congress; five of whom Congress shall appoint and commission to serve as aforesaid; and, whenever a vacancy shall happen in the council, by death or removal from office, the house of representatives shall nominate two persons, qualified as aforesaid, for each vacancy, and return their names to Congress; one of whom Congress shall appoint and commission for the residue of the term. . . .

And the governor, legislative council, and house of representatives shall have authority to make laws, in all cases, for the good government of the district, not repugnant to the principles and articles in this ordinance established and declared. And all bills, having passed by a majority in the house, and by a majority in the council, shall be referred to the governor for his assent. . . .

And, for extending the fundamental principles of civil and religious liberty, which form the basis whereon these republics, their laws, and constitutions are erected; to fix and establish those principles as the basis of all laws, constitutions, and governments, which forever hereafter shall be formed in the said territory; to provide also for the establishment of states, and permanent government therein, and for their admission to a share in the federal councils on an equal footing with the original states, at as early periods as may be consistent with the general interest:

It is hereby ordained and declared by the authority aforesaid, That the following articles shall be considered as articles of compact between the original states and the people and states in the said territory, and forever remain unalterable, unless by common consent, to wit:

ARTICLE I

No person, demeaning himself in a peaceable and orderly manner, shall ever be molested on account of his mode of worship or religious sentiments in the said territory.

ARTICLE II

The inhabitants of the said territory shall always be entitled to the benefits of the writ of habeas corpus and of the trial by jury; of a proportionate representation of the people in the legislature; and of judicial proceedings according to the course of the common law. All persons shall be bailable, unless for capital offenses, where the proof shall be evident, or the presumption great. All fines shall be moderate; and no cruel or unusual punishments shall be inflicted. No man shall be deprived of his liberty or property, but by the judgment of his peers or the law of the land. . . .

ARTICLE III

Religion, morality, and knowledge being necessary to good government and the happiness of mankind, schools and the means of education shall forever be encouraged. The utmost good faith shall always be observed toward the Indians; their lands and property shall never be taken from them without their consent; and in their property, rights, and liberty they shall never be invaded or disturbed unless in just and lawful wars authorized by Congress; but laws founded in justice and humanity shall from time to time be made for preventing wrongs being done to them, and for preserving peace and friendship with them.

ARTICLE IV

The said territory, and the states which may be formed therein, shall forever remain a part of this confederacy of the United States of America, subject to the Articles of Confederation, and to such alterations therein as shall be constitutionally made; and to all the acts and ordinances of the United States in Congress assembled, conformable thereto.

The inhabitants and settlers in the said territory shall be subject to pay a part of the federal debts contracted, or to be contracted, and a proportional part of the expenses of government to be apportioned on them by Congress, according to the same common rule and measure by which apportionments thereof shall be made on other states; and the taxes for paying their proportion shall be laid and levied by the authority and direction of the legislatures of the district or districts, or new states, as in the original states, within the time agreed upon by the United States in Congress assembled. . . .

The navigable waters leading into the Mississippi and St. Lawrence, and the carrying places between the same, shall be common highways and forever free, as well to the inhabitants of the said territory as to the citizens of the United States, and those of any other states that may be admitted into the confederacy, without any tax, impost, or duty therefor.

ARTICLE V

There shall be formed in the said territory not less than three nor more than five states; and the boundaries of the states, as soon as Virginia shall alter her act of cession and consent to the same, shall become fixed and established as follows, to wit: The western state, in the said territory, shall be bounded by the Mississippi, the Ohio, and Wabash rivers; a direct line drawn from the Wabash and Post Vincents due north to the territorial line between the United States and Canada; and, by the said territorial line, to the Lake of the Woods and Mississippi. The middle state shall be bounded by the said direct line, the Wabash from Post Vincents to the Ohio, by the Ohio, by a direct line drawn due north from the mouth of the Great Miami to the said territorial line, and by the said territorial line. The eastern state shall be bounded by the last mentioned direct line, the Ohio, Pennsylvania, and the said territorial line.

Provided, however, And it is further understood and declared that the boundaries of these three states shall be subject so far to be altered, that, if Congress shall hereafter find it expedient, they shall have authority to form one or two states in that part of the said territory which lies north of an east-and-west line drawn through the southerly bend or extreme of Lake Michigan. And whenever any of the said states shall have sixty thousand free inhabitants therein, such state shall be admitted, by its delegates, into the Congress of the United States on an equal footing with the original states, in all respects whatever; and shall be at liberty to form a permanent constitution and state government:

Provided, The constitution and government so to be formed shall be republican, and in conformity to the principles contained in these articles; and, so far as it can be consistent with the general interest of the confederacy, such admission shall be allowed at an earlier period, and when there may be a less number of free inhabitants in the state than sixty thousand.

ARTICLE VI

There shall be neither slavery nor involuntary servitude in the said territory, otherwise than in punishment of crimes whereof the party shall have been duly convicted: *Provided, always,* That any person escaping into the same, from whom labor or service is lawfully claimed in any one of the original states, such fugitive may be lawfully reclaimed, and conveyed to the person claiming his or her labor or services as aforesaid.

Be it ordained by the authority aforesaid, That the resolutions of the twenty-third of April 1784, relative to the subject of this ordinance, be, and the same are hereby repealed and declared null and void.

ON THE CONSTITUTION

To the people of the state of New York: In reviewing the defects of the existing Confederation, and showing that they cannot be supplied by a government of less energy than that before the public, several of the most important principles of the latter fell of course under consideration. But as the ultimate object of these papers is to determine clearly and fully the merits of this Constitution, and the expediency of adopting it, our plan cannot be complete without taking a more critical and thorough survey of the work of the convention, without examining it on all its sides, comparing it in all its parts, and calculating its probable effects.

That this remaining task may be executed under impressions conducive to a just and fair result, some reflections must in this place be indulged, which candor previously suggests.

It is a misfortune, inseparable from human affairs, that public measures are rarely investigated with that spirit of moderation which is essential to a just estimate of their real tendency to advance or obstruct the public good; and that this spirit is more apt to be diminished than promoted, by those occasions which require an unusual exercise of it. To those who have been led by experience to attend to this consideration, it could not appear surprising, that the act of the convention, which recommends so many important changes and innovations, which may be viewed in so many lights and relations, and which touches the springs of so many passions and interests, should find or excite dispositions unfriendly, both on one side and on the other, to a fair discussion and accurate judgment of its merits. . . .

The novelty of the undertaking immediately strikes us. It has been shown in the course of these papers that the existing Confederation is founded on principles which are fallacious; that we must consequently change this first foundation, and with it the superstructure resting upon it. It has been shown that the other confederacies which could be consulted as precedents have been vitiated by the same erroneous principles and can therefore furnish no other light than that of beacons, which give warning of the course to be shunned, without pointing out that which ought to be pursued. The most that the convention could do in such a situation was to avoid the errors suggested by the past experience of other countries, as well as of our own, and to provide a convenient mode of rectifying their own errors, as future experience may unfold them.

Among the difficulties encountered by the convention, a very important one must have lain in combining the requisite stability and energy in government, with the inviolable attention due to liberty and to the republican form. Without substantially accomplishing this part of their undertaking, they would have very imperfectly fulfilled the object of their appointment, or the expectation of the public; yet that it could not be easily accomplished will be denied by no one who is unwilling to betray his ignorance of the subject. Energy in government is essential to that security against external and internal danger and to that prompt and salutary execution of the laws which enter into the very definition of good government. Stability in government is essential to national character and to the advantages annexed to it, as well as to that repose and confidence in the minds of the people, which are among the chief blessings of civil society. An irregular and mutable legislation is not more an evil in itself than it is odious to the people; and it may be pronounced with assurance that the people of this country, enlightened as they are with regard to the nature, and interested, as the great body of them are, in the effects of good government, will never be satisfied till some remedy be applied to the vicissitudes and uncertainties which characterize the state administrations. On comparing, however, these valuable ingredients with the vital principles of liberty, we must perceive at once the difficulty of mingling them together in their due proportions. The genius of republican liberty seems to demand on one side, not only that all power should be derived from the people, but that those entrusted with it should be kept in dependence on the people, by a short duration of their appointments and that even during this short period the trust should be placed not in a few, but a number of hands. Stability, on the contrary, requires that the hands in which power is lodged should continue for a length of time the same. A frequent change of men will result from a frequent return of elections; and a frequent change of measures from a frequent change of men; whilst energy in government requires not only a certain duration of power but the execution of it by a single hand.

How far the convention may have succeeded in this part of their work will better appear on a more accurate view of it. From the cursory view here taken, it must clearly appear to have been an arduous part.

Not less arduous must have been the task of marking the proper line of partition between the authority of the general and that of the state governments. . . . Experience has instructed us that no skill in the science of government has yet been able to discriminate and define, with sufficient certainty, its three great provinces—the legislative, executive, and judiciary; or even the privileges and powers of the different legislative branches. Questions daily occur in the course of practice, which prove the obscurity which reigns in these subjects and which puzzle the greatest adepts in political science.

The experience of ages, with the continued and combined labors of the most enlightened legislators and jurists, has been equally unsuccessful in delineating the several objects and limits of different codes of laws and different tribunals of justice. The precise extent of the common law, and the statute law, the maritime law, the ecclesiastical law, the law of corporations, and other local laws and customs, remains still to be clearly and finally established in Great Britain, where accuracy in such subjects has been more industriously pursued than in any other part of the world. The jurisdiction of her several courts, general and local, of law, of equity, of admiralty, etc., is not less a source of frequent and intricate discussions, sufficiently denoting the indeterminate limits by which they are respectively circumscribed.

All new laws, though penned with the greatest technical skill, and passed on the fullest and most mature deliberation, are considered as more or less obscure and equivocal, until their meaning be liquidated and ascertained by a series of particular discussions and adjudications. Besides the obscurity arising from the complexity of objects, and the imperfection of the human faculties, the medium through which the conceptions of men are conveyed to each other adds a fresh embarrassment. The use of words is to express ideas. Perspicuity, therefore, requires not only that the ideas should be distinctly formed, but that they should be expressed by words distinctly and exclusively appropriate to them. But no language is so copious as to supply words and phrases for every complex idea, or so correct as not to include many equivocally denoting different ideas. . . .

Here, then, are three sources of vague and incorrect definitions: indistinctness of the object, imperfection of the organ of conception, inadequateness of the vehicle of ideas. Any one of these must produce a certain degree of obscurity. The convention, in delineating the boundary between the federal and state jurisdictions, must have experienced the full effect of them all.

To the difficulties already mentioned may be added the interfering pretensions of the larger and smaller states. We cannot err in supposing that the former would contend for a participation in the government, fully proportioned to their superior wealth and importance; and that the latter would not be less tenacious of the equality at present enjoyed by them. We may well suppose that neither side would entirely yield to the other, and consequently that the struggle could be terminated only by compromise. It is extremely probable, also, that after the ratio of representation had been adjusted, this very compromise must have produced a fresh struggle between the same parties, to give such a turn to the organization of the government, and to the distribution of its powers, as would increase the importance of the branches, in forming which they had respectively obtained the greatest share of influence. There are features in the Constitution which warrant each of these suppositions; and as far as either of them is well founded, it shows that the convention must have been compelled to sacrifice theoretical propriety to the force of extraneous considerations.

Nor could it have been the large and small states only, which would marshal themselves in opposition to each other on various points. Other combinations, resulting from a difference of local position and policy, must have created additional difficulties. As every state may be divided into different districts, and its citizens into different classes, which give birth to contending interests and local jealousies, so the different parts of the United States are distinguished from each other by a variety of circumstances, which produce a like effect on a larger scale. And although this variety of interests, for reasons sufficiently explained in a former paper, may have a salutary influence on the administration of the government when formed, yet every one must be sensible of the contrary influence, which must have been experienced in the task of forming it.

Would it be wonderful if, under the pressure of all these difficulties, the convention should have been forced into some deviations from that artificial structure and regular symmetry which an abstract view of the subject might lead an ingenious theorist to bestow on a Constitution planned in his closet or in his imagination? The real wonder is that so many difficulties should have been surmounted, and surmounted with a unanimity almost as unprecedented as it must have been unexpected. . . .

We had occasion, in a former paper, to take notice of the repeated trials which have been unsuccessfully made in the United Netherlands for reforming the baneful and notorious vices of their constitution. The history of almost all the great councils and consultations held among mankind for reconciling their discordant opinions, assuaging their mutual jealousies, and adjusting their respective interests, is a history of factions, contentions, and disappointments and may be classed among the most dark and degraded pictures which display the infirmities and depravities of the human character. If, in a few scattered instances, a brighter aspect is presented, they serve only as exceptions to admonish us of the general truth; and by their luster to darken the gloom of the adverse prospect to which they are contrasted. In revolving the causes from which these exceptions result, and applying them to the particular instances before us, we are necessarily led to two important conclusions. The first is that the convention must have enjoyed, in a very singular degree, an exemption from the pestilential influence of party animosities—the disease most incident to deliberative bodies and most apt to contaminate their proceedings. The second conclusion is that all the deputations composing the convention were satisfactorily accommodated by the final act, or were induced to accede to it by a deep conviction of the necessity of sacrificing private opinions and partial interests to the public good, and by a despair of seeing this necessity diminished by delays or by new experiments.

JAMES MADISON,
from *The Federalist*, 1788

THE CONSTITUTION OF THE UNITED STATES

June 21, 1788

We the people of the United States, in order to form a more perfect union, establish justice, insure domestic tranquillity, provide for the common defense, promote the general welfare, and secure the blessings of liberty to ourselves and our posterity, do ordain and establish this Constitution for the United States of America.

ARTICLE I

SECTION 1. All legislative powers herein granted shall be vested in a Congress of the United States, which shall consist of a Senate and House of Representatives.

SECTION 2. The House of Representatives shall be composed of members chosen every second year by the people of the several states, and the electors in each state shall have the qualifications requisite for electors of the most numerous branch of the state legislature.

No person shall be a representative who shall not have attained to the age of twenty-five years, and been seven years a citizen of the United States, and who shall not, when elected, be an inhabitant of that state in which he shall be chosen.

Representatives and direct taxes shall be apportioned among the several states which may be included within this Union, according to their respective numbers, which shall be determined by adding to the whole number of free persons, including those bound to service for a term of years, and excluding Indians not taxed, three-fifths of all other persons. The actual enumeration shall be made within three years after the first meeting of the Congress of the United States, and within every subsequent term of ten years, in such manner as they shall by law direct. The number of representatives shall not exceed one for every thirty thousand, but each state shall have at least one representative; and until such enumeration shall be made, the state of New Hampshire shall be entitled to choose three, Massachusetts eight, Rhode Island and Providence Plantations one, Connecticut five, New York six, New Jersey four, Pennsylvania eight, Delaware one, Maryland six, Virginia ten, North Carolina five, South Carolina five, and Georgia three.

When vacancies happen in the representation from any state, the executive authority thereof shall issue writs of election to fill such vacancies.

The House of Representatives shall choose their speaker and other officers; and shall have the sole power of impeachment.

SECTION 3. The Senate of the United States shall be composed of two senators from each state, chosen by the legislature thereof, for six years; and each senator shall have one vote.

Immediately after they shall be assembled in consequence of the first election, they shall be divided as equally as may be into three classes. The seats of the senators of the first class shall be vacated at the expiration of the second year, of the second class at the expiration of the fourth year, and of the third class at the expiration of the sixth year, so that one third may be chosen every second year; and if vacancies happen by resignation, or otherwise, during the recess of the legislature of any state, the executive thereof may make temporary appointments until the next meeting of the legislature, which shall then fill such vacancies.

No person shall be a senator who shall not have attained to the age of thirty years, and been nine years a citizen of the United States, and who shall not, when elected, be an inhabitant of that state for which he shall be chosen.

The vice president of the United States shall be president of the Senate, but shall have no vote, unless they be equally divided.

The Senate shall choose their other officers, and also a president pro tempore, in the absence of the vice president, or when he shall exercise the office of president of the United States.

The Senate shall have the sole power to try all impeachments. When sitting for that purpose, they shall be on oath or affirmation. When the president of the United States is tried, the chief justice shall preside: and no person shall be convicted without the concurrence of two-thirds of the members present.

Judgment in cases of impeachment shall not extend further than to removal from office, and disqualification to hold and enjoy any office of honor, trust or profit under the United States: but the party convicted shall nevertheless be liable and subject to indictment, trial, judgment, and punishment, according to law.

SECTION 4. The times, places, and manner of holding elections for senators and representatives shall be prescribed in each state by the legislature thereof; but the Congress may at any time by law make or alter such regulations, except as to the places of choosing senators.

The Congress shall assemble at least once in every year, and such meeting shall be on the first Monday in December, unless they shall by law appoint a different day.

SECTION 5. Each House shall be the judge of the elections, returns, and qualifications of its own members, and a majority of each shall constitute a quorum to do business; but a smaller number may adjourn from day to day, and may be authorized to compel the attendance of absent members, in such manner, and under such penalties as each House may provide.

Each House may determine the rules of its proceedings, punish its members for disorderly behavior, and, with the concurrence of two-thirds, expel a member.

Each House shall keep a journal of its proceedings, and from time to time publish the same, excepting such parts as may in their judgment require secrecy; and the yeas and nays of the members of either House on any question shall, at the desire of one-fifth of those present, be entered on the journal.

Neither House, during the session of Congress, shall, without the consent of the other, adjourn for more than three days, nor to any other place than that in which the two Houses shall be sitting.

SECTION 6. The senators and representatives shall receive a compensation for their services, to be ascertained by law, and paid out of the Treasury of the United States. They shall in all cases, except treason, felony, and breach of the peace, be privileged from arrest during their attendance at the session of their respective Houses, and in going to and returning from the same; and for any speech or debate in either House, they shall not be questioned in any other place.

No senator or representative shall, during the time for which he was elected, be appointed to any civil office under the authority of the United States, which shall have been created, or the emoluments whereof shall have been increased during such time; and no person holding any office under the United States shall be a member of either House during his continuance in office.

SECTION 7. All bills for raising revenue shall originate in the House of Representatives; but the Senate may propose or concur with amendments as on other bills.

Every bill which shall have passed the House of Representatives and the Senate, shall, before it become a law, be presented to the president of the United States; if he approve he shall sign it, but if not he shall return it, with his objections to that House in which it shall have originated, who shall enter the objections at large on their journal, and proceed to reconsider it. If after such reconsideration two-thirds of that House shall agree to pass the bill, it shall be sent, together with the objections, to the other House, by which it shall likewise be reconsidered, and if approved by two-thirds of that House, it shall become a law. But in all such cases the votes of both Houses shall be determined by yeas and nays, and the names of the persons voting for and against the bill shall be entered on the journal of each House respectively. If any bill shall not be returned by the president within ten days (Sundays excepted) after it shall have been presented to him, the same shall be a law, in like manner as if he had signed it, unless the Congress by their adjournment prevent its return, in which case it shall not be a law.

Every order, resolution, or vote to which the concurrence of the Senate and House of Representatives may be necessary (except on a question of adjournment) shall be presented to the president of the United States; and before the same shall take effect, shall be approved by him, or being disapproved by him, shall be repassed by two-thirds of the Senate and House of Representatives, according to the rules and limitations prescribed in the case of a bill.

SECTION 8. The Congress shall have power to lay and collect taxes, duties, imposts, and excises, to pay the debts and provide for the common defense and general welfare of the United States; but all duties, imposts, and excises shall be uniform throughout the United States,

To borrow money on the credit of the United States;

To regulate commerce with foreign nations, and among the several states, and with the Indian tribes;

To establish an uniform rule of naturalization, and uniform laws on the subject of bankruptcies throughout the United States;

To coin money, regulate the value thereof, and of foreign coin, and fix the standard of weights and measures;

To provide for the punishment of counterfeiting the securities and current coin of the United States;

To establish post offices and post roads;

To promote the progress of science and useful arts, by securing for limited times to authors and inventors the exclusive right to their respective writings and discoveries;

To constitute tribunals inferior to the Supreme Court;

To define and punish piracies and felonies committed on the high seas, and offenses against the law of nations;

To declare war, grant letters of marque and reprisal, and make rules concerning captures on land and water;

To raise and support armies, but no appropriation of money to that use shall be for a longer term than two years;

To provide and maintain a navy;

To make rules for the government and regulation of the land and naval forces;

To provide for calling forth the militia to execute the laws of the Union, suppress insurrections, and repel invasions;

To provide for organizing, arming, and disciplining the militia, and for governing such part of them as may be employed in the service of the United States, reserving to the states respectively, the appointment of the officers, and the authority of training the militia according to the discipline prescribed by Congress;

To exercise exclusive legislation in all cases whatsoever, over such district (not exceeding ten miles square) as may, by cession of particular states, and the acceptance of Congress, become the seat of the government of the United States, and to exercise like authority over all places purchased by the consent of the legislature of the state in which the same shall be, for the erection of forts, magazines, arsenals, dockyards, and other needful buildings; and,

To make all laws which shall be necessary and proper for carrying into execution the foregoing powers, and all other powers vested by this Constitution in the government of the United States, or in any department or officer thereof.

SECTION 9. The migration or importation of such persons as any of the states now existing shall think proper to admit, shall not be prohibited by the Congress prior to the year one thousand eight hundred and eight, but a tax or duty may be imposed on such importation, not exceeding ten dollars for each person.

The privilege of the writ of habeas corpus shall not be suspended, unless when in cases of rebellion or invasion the public safety may require it.

No bill of attainder or ex post facto law shall be passed.

No capitation, or other direct, tax shall be laid, unless in proportion to the census or enumeration herein before directed to be taken.

No tax or duty shall be laid on articles exported from any state.

No preference shall be given by any regulation of commerce or revenue to the ports of one state over those of another; nor shall vessels bound to, or from, one state, be obliged to enter, clear, or pay duties in another.

No money shall be drawn from the Treasury, but in consequence of appropriations made by law; and a regular statement and account of the receipts and expenditures of all public money shall be published from time to time.

No title of nobility shall be granted by the United States: and no person holding any office of profit or trust under them, shall, without the consent of the Congress, accept of any present, emolument, office, or title, of any kind whatever, from any king, prince, or foreign state.

SECTION 10. No state shall enter into any treaty, alliance, or confederation; grant letters of marque and reprisal; coin money; emit bills of credit; make anything but gold and silver coin a tender in payment of debts; pass any bill of attainder, ex post facto law, or law impairing the obligation of contracts; or grant any title of nobility.

No state shall, without the consent of the Congress, lay any imposts or duties on imports or exports, except what may be absolutely necessary for executing its inspection laws: and the net produce of all duties and imposts, laid by any state on imports or exports, shall be for the use of the Treasury of the United States; and all such laws shall be subject to the revision and control of the Congress.

No state shall, without the consent of Congress, lay any duty of tonnage, keep troops or ships of war in time of peace, enter into any agreement or compact with another state or with a foreign power, or engage in war, unless actually invaded, or in such imminent danger as will not admit of delay.

ARTICLE II

SECTION 1. The executive power shall be vested in a president of the United States of America. He shall hold his office during the term of four years, and, together with the vice president, chosen for the same term, be elected, as follows.

Each state shall appoint, in such manner as the legislature thereof may direct, a number of electors, equal to the whole number of senators and representatives to which the state may be entitled in the Congress: but no senator or representative, or person holding an office of trust or profit under the United States, shall be appointed an elector.

The electors shall meet in their respective states, and vote by ballot for two persons, of whom one at least shall not be an inhabitant of the same state with themselves. And they shall make a list of all the persons voted for, and of the number of votes for each; which list they shall sign and certify, and transmit sealed to the seat of the government of the United States, directed to the president of the Senate. The president of the Senate shall, in the presence of the Senate and House of Representatives, open all the certificates, and the votes shall then be counted. The person having the greatest number of votes shall be the president, if such number be a majority of the whole number of electors appointed; and if there be more than one who have such majority, and have an equal number of votes, then the House of Representatives shall immediately choose by ballot one of them for president; and if no person have a majority, then from the five highest on the list the said House shall in like manner choose the president. But in choosing the president, the votes shall be taken by states, the representation from each state having one vote; a quorum for this purpose shall consist of a member or members from two-thirds of the states, and a majority of all the states shall be necessary to a choice. In every case, after the choice of the president, the person having the greatest number of votes of the electors shall be the vice president. But if there should remain two or more who have equal votes, the Senate shall choose from them by ballot the vice president.

The Congress may determine the time of choosing the electors, and the day on which they shall give their votes; which day shall be the same throughout the United States.

No person except a natural-born citizen, or a citizen of the United States at the time of the adoption of this Constitution, shall be eligible to the office of president; neither shall any person be eligible to that office who shall not have attained to the age of thirty-five years, and been fourteen years a resident within the United States.

In case of the removal of the president from office, or of his death, resignation, or inability to discharge the powers and duties of the said office, the same shall devolve on the vice president, and the Congress may by law provide for the case of removal, death, resignation, or inability, both of the president and vice president, declaring what officer shall then act as president, and such officer shall act accordingly, until the disability be removed, or a president shall be elected.

The president shall, at stated times, receive for his services, a compensation, which shall neither be increased nor diminished during the period for which he shall have been elected, and he shall not receive within that period any other emolument from the United States, or any of them.

Before he enter on the execution of his office, he shall take the following oath or affirmation: "I do solemnly swear (or affirm) that I will faithfully execute the office of president of the United States, and will to the best of my ability, preserve, protect, and defend the Constitution of the United States."

SECTION 2. The president shall be commander in chief of the army and navy of the United States, and of the militia of the several states, when called into the actual service of the United States; he may require the opinion, in writing, of the principal officer in each of the executive departments, upon any subject relating to the duties of their respective offices, and he shall have power to grant reprieves and pardons for offenses against the United States, except in cases of impeachment.

He shall have power, by and with the advice and consent of the Senate, to make treaties, provided two-thirds of the senators present concur; and he shall nominate, and by and with the advice and consent of the Senate, shall appoint ambassadors, other public ministers and consuls, judges of the Supreme Court, and all other officers of the United States, whose appointments are not herein otherwise provided for, and which shall be established by law: but the Congress may by law vest the appointment of such inferior officers, as they think proper, in the president alone, in the courts of law, or in the heads of departments.

The president shall have power to fill up all vacancies that may happen during the recess of the Senate, by granting commissions which shall expire at the end of their next session.

SECTION 3. He shall from time to time give to the Congress information of the state of the Union, and recommend to their consideration such measures as he shall judge necessary and expedient, he may, on extraordinary occasions, convene both Houses, or either of them, and in case of disagreement between them, with respect to the time of adjournment, he may adjourn them to such time as he shall think proper; he shall receive ambassadors and other public ministers; he shall take care that the laws be faithfully executed, and shall commission all the officers of the United States.

SECTION 4. The president, vice president, and all civil officers of the United States shall be removed from office on impeachment for, and conviction of, treason, bribery, or other high crimes and misdemeanors.

ARTICLE III

SECTION 1. The judicial power of the United States shall be vested in one Supreme Court, and in such inferior courts as the

Congress may from time to time ordain and establish. The judges, both of the supreme and inferior courts, shall hold their offices during good behavior, and shall, at stated times, receive for their services, a compensation, which shall not be diminished during their continuance in office.

SECTION 2. The judicial power shall extend to all cases, in law and equity, arising under this Constitution, the laws of the United States, and treaties made, or which shall be made, under their authority; to all cases affecting ambassadors, other public ministers and consuls; to all cases of admiralty and maritime jurisdiction; to controversies to which the United States shall be a party; to controversies between two or more states—between a state and citizens of another state—between citizens of different states—between citizens of the same state claiming lands under grants of different states, and between a state, or the citizens thereof, and foreign states, citizens, or subjects.

In all cases affecting ambassadors, other public ministers and consuls, and those in which a state shall be party, the Supreme Court shall have original jurisdiction. In all the other cases before mentioned, the Supreme Court shall have appellate jurisdiction, both as to law and fact, with such exceptions, and under such regulations as the Congress shall make.

The trial of all crimes, except in cases of impeachment, shall be by jury; and such trial shall be held in the state where the said crimes shall have been committed; but when not committed within any state, the trial shall be at such place or places as the Congress may by law have directed.

SECTION 3. Treason against the United States shall consist only in levying war against them, or in adhering to their enemies, giving them aid and comfort. No person shall be convicted of treason unless on the testimony of two witnesses to the same overt act, or on confession in open court.

The Congress shall have power to declare the punishment of treason, but no attainder of treason shall work corruption of blood, or forfeiture except during the life of the person attainted.

ARTICLE IV

SECTION 1. Full faith and credit shall be given in each state to the public acts, records, and judicial proceedings of every other state. And the Congress may by general laws prescribe the manner in which such acts, records, and proceedings shall be proved, and the effect thereof.

SECTION 2. The citizens of each state shall be entitled to all privileges and immunities of citizens in the several states.

A person charged in any state with treason, felony, or other crime, who shall flee from justice, and be found in another state, shall on demand of the executive authority of the state from which he fled, be delivered up, to be removed to the state having jurisdiction of the crime.

No person held to service or labor in one state, under the laws thereof, escaping into another, shall, in consequence of any law or regulation therein, be discharged from such service or labor, but shall be delivered up on claim of the party to whom such service or labor may be due.

SECTION 3. New states may be admitted by the Congress into this Union; but no new state shall be formed or erected within the jurisdiction of any other state; nor any state be formed by the junction of two or more states, or parts of states, without the consent of the legislatures of the states concerned as well as of the Congress.

The Congress shall have power to dispose of and make all needful rules and regulations respecting the territory or other property belonging to the United States; and nothing in this Constitution shall be so construed as to prejudice any claims of the United States, or of any particular state.

SECTION 4. The United States shall guarantee to every state in this Union a republican form of government, and shall protect each of them against invasion; and on application of the legislature, or of the executive (when the legislature cannot be convened) against domestic violence.

ARTICLE V

The Congress, whenever two-thirds of both Houses shall deem it necessary, shall propose amendments to this Constitution, or, on the application of the legislatures of two-thirds of the several states, shall call a convention for proposing amendments, which, in either case, shall be valid to all intents and purposes, as part of this Constitution, when ratified by the legislatures of three-fourths of the several states, or by conventions in three-fourths thereof, as the one or the other mode of ratification may be proposed by the Congress; provided that no amendment which may be made prior to the year one thousand eight hundred and eight shall in any manner affect the first and fourth clauses in the ninth section of the first article; and that no state, without its consent, shall be deprived of its equal suffrage in the Senate.

ARTICLE VI

All debts contracted and engagements entered into, before the adoption of this Constitution, shall be as valid against the United States under this Constitution, as under the Confederation.

This Constitution, and the laws of the United States which shall be made in pursuance thereof, and all treaties made, or which shall be made, under the authority of the United States, shall be the supreme law of the land; and the judges in every state shall be bound thereby, anything in the constitution or laws of any state to the contrary notwithstanding.

The senators and representatives before mentioned, and the members of the several state legislatures, and all executive and judicial officers, both of the United States and of the several states, shall be bound by oath or affirmation, to support this Constitution; but no religious test shall ever be required as a qualification to any office or public trust under the United States.

ARTICLE VII

The ratification of the conventions of nine states shall be sufficient for the establishment of this Constitution between the states so ratifying the same.

Done in convention by the unanimous consent of the states present the seventeenth day of September in the year of Our Lord one thousand seven hundred and eighty-seven and of the Independence of the United States of America the twelfth. In witness whereof we have hereunto subscribed our names.

THE BILL OF RIGHTS

The First Ten Amendments to the Constitution of the United States, Adopted December 15, 1791

ARTICLE I

Congress shall make no law respecting an establishment of religion, or prohibiting the free exercise thereof; or abridging the freedom of speech, or of the press; or the right of the people peaceably to assemble, and to petition the government for a redress of grievances.

ARTICLE II

A well-regulated militia, being necessary to the security of a free state, the right of the people to keep and bear arms, shall not be infringed.

ARTICLE III

No soldier shall, in time of peace be quartered in any house, without the consent of the owner, nor in time of war, but in a manner to be prescribed by law.

ARTICLE IV

The right of the people to be secure in their persons, houses, papers, and effects, against unreasonable searches and seizures, shall not be violated, and no warrants shall issue, but upon probable cause, supported by oath or affirmation, and particularly describing the place to be searched, and the persons or things to be seized.

ARTICLE V

No person shall be held to answer for a capital, or otherwise infamous crime, unless on a presentment or indictment of a grand jury, except in cases arising in the land or naval forces, or in the militia, when in actual service in time of war or public danger; nor shall any person be subject for the same offense to be twice put in jeopardy of life or limb; nor shall be compelled in any criminal case to be a witness against himself, nor be deprived of life, liberty, or property, without due process of law; nor shall private property be taken for public use, without just compensation.

ARTICLE VI

In all criminal prosecutions, the accused shall enjoy the right to a speedy and public trial, by an impartial jury of the state and district wherein the crime shall have been committed, which district shall have been previously ascertained by law, and to be informed of the nature and cause of the accusation; to be confronted with the witnesses against him; to have compulsory process for obtaining witnesses in his favor, and to have the assistance of counsel for his defense.

ARTICLE VII

In suits at common law, where the value in controversy shall exceed twenty dollars, the right of trial by jury shall be preserved, and no fact tried by a jury shall be otherwise reexamined in any court of the United States, than according to the rules of the common law.

ARTICLE VIII

Excessive bail shall not be required, nor excessive fines imposed, nor cruel and unusual punishments inflicted.

ARTICLE IX

The enumeration in the Constitution, of certain rights, shall not be construed to deny or disparage others retained by the people.

ARTICLE X

The powers not delegated to the United States by the Constitution, nor prohibited by it to the states, are reserved to the states respectively, or to the people.

PART TWO

★

North and South

THE ISSUES of social and states' rights that led to the Civil War smoldered since the republic's creation, when the controversy about slavery had been deeply divisive. One of the first legislative tests of the uneasy truce came in the Missouri Compromise, which admitted Missouri as a slave-holding state, prohibited slavery in the remaining areas that comprised the Louisiana Purchase, and welcomed Maine as a free state. Abraham Lincoln, even as he debated with Stephen A. Douglas and ran against him in the 1858 Illinois U.S. Senate election, became the symbol of the inevitable clash. Lincoln's election as president was the spark that ignited war and set the stage for the final, and tragic, settlement of the slavery question.

South Carolina seceded from the Union in December 1860, and within months the Confederacy was born and war broke out. The horrors of the Civil War inspired poetry both immediately and for years afterward. In 1861 Julia Ward Howe wrote what became recognized as the anthem of the Northern cause, the "Battle Hymn of the Republic." In their poems, such major writers as John Greenleaf Whittier, Herman Melville, and Bret Harte described the agony and heroism of individual battles. And Abraham Lincoln, whose assassination reinforced his stature as the personification of the war's agony, continued to be the subject of verse for decades, from Walt Whitman's "O Captain! My Captain!" to Vachel Lindsay's "Abraham Lincoln Walks at Midnight."

THE MISSOURI COMPROMISE

MISSOURI ENABLING ACT

March 6, 1820

An act to authorize the people of the Missouri Territory to form a constitution and state government, and for the admission of such state into the Union on an equal footing with the original states, and to prohibit slavery in certain territories.

Be it enacted, That the inhabitants of that portion of the Missouri Territory included within the boundaries hereinafter designated, be, and they are hereby authorized to form for themselves a constitution and state government, and to assume such name as they shall deem proper; and the said state, when formed, shall be admitted into the Union, upon an equal footing with the original states, in all respects whatsoever.

SECTION 2. That the said state shall consist of all the territory included within the following boundaries, to wit: Beginning in the middle of the Mississippi River, on the parallel of thirty-six degrees of north latitude; thence west, along that parallel of latitude, to the St. Francois River; thence up, and following the course of that river, in the middle of the main channel thereof, to the parallel of latitude of thirty-six degrees and thirty minutes; thence west, along the same, to a point where the said parallel is intersected by a meridian line passing through the middle of the mouth of the Kansas River, where the same empties into the Missouri River, thence, from the point aforesaid north, along the said meridian line, to the intersection of the parallel of latitude which passes through the rapids of the river Des Moines, making the said line to correspond with the Indian boundary line; thence east, from the point of intersection last aforesaid, along the said parallel of latitude, to the middle of the channel of the main fork of the said river Des Moines; thence down and along the middle of the main channel of the said river Des Moines, to the mouth of the same, where it empties into the

Mississippi River; thence, due east, to the middle of the main channel of the Mississippi River; thence down, and following the course of the Mississippi River, in the middle of the main channel thereof, to the place of beginning. . . .

SECTION 3. That all free white male citizens of the United States, who shall have arrived at the age of twenty-one years, and have resided in said territory three months previous to the day of election, and all other persons qualified to vote for representatives to the general assembly of the said territory, shall be qualified to be elected, and they are hereby qualified and authorized to vote, and choose representatives to form a convention. . . .

SECTION 8. That in all that territory ceded by France to the United States, under the name of Louisiana, which lies north of thirty-six degrees and thirty minutes north latitude, not included within the limits of the state contemplated by this act, slavery and involuntary servitude, otherwise than in the punishment of crimes whereof the parties shall have been duly convicted, shall be, and is hereby, forever prohibited: *Provided always,* That any person escaping into the same, from whom labor or service is lawfully claimed, in any state or territory of the United States, such fugitive may be lawfully reclaimed and conveyed to the person claiming his or her labor or service as aforesaid.

THE CONSTITUTION OF MISSOURI

July 19, 1820

SECTION 26. The general assembly shall not have power to pass laws:

1. For the emancipation of slaves without the consent of their owners; or without paying them, before such emancipation, a full equivalent for such slaves so emancipated; and,

2. To prevent bonafide immigrants to this state, or actual settlers therein, from bringing from any of the United States, or from any of their territories, such persons as may there be

deemed to be slaves, so long as any persons of the same description are allowed to be held as slaves by the laws of this state.

They shall have power to pass laws:

1. To prevent bonafide immigrants to this state of any slaves who may have committed any high crime in any other state or territory;

2. To prohibit the introduction of any slave for the purpose of speculation, or as an article of trade or merchandise;

3. To prohibit the introduction of any slave, or the offspring of any slave, who heretofore may have been, or who hereafter may be, imported from any foreign country into the United States, or any territory thereof, in contravention of any existing statute of the United States; and,

4. To permit the owners of slaves to emancipate them, saving the right of creditors, where the person so emancipating will give security that the slave so emancipated shall not become a public charge.

It shall be their duty, as soon as may be, to pass such laws as may be necessary:

1. To prevent free Negroes . . . [and] mulattoes from coming to and settling in this state, under any pretext whatsoever; and,

2. To oblige the owners of slaves to treat them with humanity, and to abstain from all injuries to them extending to life or limb.

A House Divided

*Abraham Lincoln's Speech at the Republican State
Convention, Springfield, Illinois, June 7, 1858*

Mr. President and Gentlemen of the Convention: If we could first know where we are, and whither we are tending, we could better judge what to do, and how to do it. We are now far into the fifth year since a policy was initiated with the avowed object and confident promise of putting an end to slavery agitation. Under the operation of that policy, that agitation has not only not ceased but has constantly augmented. In my opinion, it will not cease until a crisis shall have been reached and passed. "A house divided against itself cannot stand." I believe this government cannot endure permanently half slave and half free. I do not expect the Union to be dissolved; I do not expect the house to fall; but I do expect it will cease to be divided. It will become all one thing, or all the other. Either the opponents of slavery will arrest the further spread of it, and place it where the public mind shall rest in the belief that it is in the course of ultimate extinction, or its advocates will push it forward till it shall become alike lawful in all the states, old as well as new, North as well as South.

Have we no tendency to the latter condition?

Let anyone who doubts carefully contemplate that now almost complete legal combination—piece of machinery, so to speak—compounded of the Nebraska doctrine and the *Dred Scott* decision. Let him consider not only what work the machinery is adapted to do, and how well adapted, but also let him study the history of its construction, and trace, if he can, or rather fail, if he can, to trace the evidences of design, and concert of action, among its chief architects, from the beginning.

The new year of 1854 found slavery excluded from more than half the states by state constitutions, and from most of the national territory by congressional prohibition. Four days later

commenced the struggle which ended in repealing that congressional prohibition. This opened all the national territory to
slavery and was the first point gained. . . .

While the Nebraska Bill was passing through Congress, a
law case, involving the question of a Negro's freedom, by reason
of his owner having voluntarily taken him first into a free state,
and then into a territory covered by the congressional prohibition, and held him as a slave for a long time in each, was passing
through the United States Circuit Court for the District of Missouri; and both Nebraska Bill and lawsuit were brought to a
decision in the same month of May 1854. The Negro's name was
Dred Scott, which name now designates the decision finally
made in the case. Before the then next presidential election, the
law case came to, and was argued in, the Supreme Court of the
United States; but the decision of it was deferred until after the
election. . . .

The election came. Mr. Buchanan was elected, and the endorsement, such as it was, secured. That was the second point
gained. . . .

The reputed author of the Nebraska Bill finds an early
occasion to make a speech at this capital endorsing the *Dred
Scott* decision, and vehemently denouncing all opposition to it.
The new president, too, seizes the early occasion of the Silliman
letter to endorse and strongly construe that decision, and to
express his astonishment that any different view had ever been
entertained! . . .

The several points of the *Dred Scott* decision, in connection
with Senator Douglas's "care not" policy, constitute the piece of
machinery, in its present state of advancement. This was the
third point gained. The working points of that machinery are:

Firstly, That no Negro slave, imported as such from Africa,
and no descendant of such slave, can ever be a citizen of any
state, in the sense of that term as used in the Constitution of the
United States. This point is made in order to deprive the Negro,
in every possible event, of the benefit of that provision of the
United States Constitution which declares that "the citizens of

each state shall be entitled to all privileges and immunities of citizens in the several states."

Secondly, That, "subject to the Constitution of the United States," neither Congress nor a territorial legislature can exclude slavery from any United States territory. This point is made in order that individual men may fill up the territories with slaves, without danger of losing them as property, and thus to enhance the chances of permanency to the institution through all the future.

Thirdly, That whether the holding a Negro in actual slavery in a free state makes him free, as against the holder, the United States courts will not decide, but will leave to be decided by the courts of any slave state the Negro may be forced into by the master. This point is made, not to be pressed immediately; but, if acquiesced in for a while, and apparently endorsed by the people at an election, then to sustain the logical conclusion that what Dred Scott's master might lawfully do with Dred Scott in the free state of Illinois, every other master may lawfully do with any other one, or one thousand slaves, in Illinois, or in any other free state. . . .

It will throw additional light on the latter, to go back and run the mind over the string of historical facts already stated. Several things will now appear less dark and mysterious than they did when they were transpiring. The people were to be left "perfectly free," "subject only to the Constitution." What the Constitution had to do with it outsiders could not then see. Plainly enough now, it was an exactly fitted niche for the *Dred Scott* decision afterward to come in and declare that perfect freedom of the people to be just no freedom at all. Why was the amendment expressly declaring the right of the people to exclude slavery voted down? Plainly enough now, the adoption of it would have spoiled the niche for the *Dred Scott* decision. Why was the court decision held up? Why even a senator's individual opinion withheld till after the presidential election? Plainly enough now, the speaking out then would have damaged the "perfectly free" argument upon which the election was to be carried. Why the outgoing president's felicitation on the endorsement? Why the delay of a reargument? Why the incoming president's advance exhortation in favor of the decision? . . .

We cannot absolutely know that all these exact adaptations are the result of preconcert. But when we see a lot of framed timbers, different portions of which we know have been gotten out at different times and places and by different workmen—Stephen, Franklin, Roger, and James, for instance—and when we see these timbers joined together, and see they exactly make the frame of a house or a mill, all the tenons and mortices exactly fitting, and all the lengths and proportions of the different pieces exactly adapted to their respective places, and not a piece too many or too few, not omitting even scaffolding—or, if a single piece be lacking, we see the place in the frame exactly fitted and prepared to yet bring such piece in—in such a case we find it impossible not to believe that Stephen and Franklin and Roger and James all understood one another from the beginning, and all worked upon a common plan or draft drawn up before the first blow was struck. . . .

While the opinion of the court, by Chief Justice Taney, in the *Dred Scott* case, and the separate opinions of all the concurring judges, expressly declare that the Constitution of the United States neither permits Congress nor a territorial legislature to exclude slavery from any United States territory, they all omit to declare whether or not the same Constitution permits a state, or the people of a state, to exclude it. . . . We may, ere long, see . . . another Supreme Court decision declaring that the Constitution of the United States does not permit a state to exclude slavery from its limits. And this may especially be expected if the doctrine of "care not whether slavery be voted down or voted up" shall gain upon the public mind sufficiently to give promise that such a decision can be maintained when made.

Such a decision is all that slavery now lacks of being alike lawful in all the states. Welcome, or unwelcome, such decision is probably coming, and will soon be upon us, unless the power of the present political dynasty shall be met and overthrown.

We shall lie down pleasantly dreaming that the people of Missouri are on the verge of making their state free, and we shall awake to the reality instead that the Supreme Court has made Illinois a slave state. To meet and overthrow the power of that dynasty is the work now before all those who would prevent that consummation. That is what we have to do. How can we best do it?

There are those who denounce us openly to their own friends, and yet whisper us softly that Senator Douglas is the aptest instrument there is with which to effect that object. They do not tell us, nor has he told us, that he wishes any such object to be effected. They wish us to infer all from the facts that he now has a little quarrel with the present head of the dynasty; and that he has regularly voted with us on a single point upon which he and we have never differed. They remind us that he is a very great man, and that the largest of us are very small ones. Let this be granted. But "a living dog is better than a dead lion." Judge Douglas, if not a dead lion for this work, is at least a caged and toothless one. . . .

Our cause, then, must be entrusted to, and conducted by, its own undoubted friends—those whose hands are free, whose hearts are in the work, who do care for the result. Two years ago the Republicans of the nation mustered over thirteen hundred thousand strong. We did this under the single impulse of resistance to a common danger, with every external circumstance against us. Of strange, discordant, and even hostile elements, we gathered from the four winds, and formed and fought the battle through, under the constant hot fire of a disciplined, proud, and pampered enemy. Did we brave all then to falter now?—now, when that same enemy is wavering, dissevered, and belligerent? The result is not doubtful. We shall not fail—if we stand firm, we shall not fail. Wise counsels may accelerate or mistakes delay it, but, sooner or later, the victory is sure to come.

THE SECESSION OF SOUTH CAROLINA FROM THE UNION: DECLARATION OF CAUSES

December 24, 1860

The people of the state of South Carolina in convention assembled, on the second day of April, A.D. 1852, declared that the frequent violations of the Constitution of the United States by the federal government, and its encroachments upon the reserved rights of the states, fully justified this state in their withdrawal from the federal Union, but in deference to the opinions and wishes of the other slaveholding states, she forbore at that time to exercise this right. Since that time these encroachments have continued to increase, and further forbearance ceases to be a virtue.

And now the state of South Carolina, having resumed her separate and equal place among nations, deems it due to herself, to the remaining United States of America, and to the nations of the world, that she should declare the immediate causes which have led to this act.

In the year 1765, that portion of the British Empire embracing Great Britain undertook to make laws for the government of that portion composed of the thirteen American colonies. A struggle for the right of self-government ensued, which resulted, on the fourth of July 1776, in a declaration by the colonies "that they are, and of right ought to be, *free and independent states;* and that, as free and independent states, they have full power to levy war, conclude peace, contract alliances, establish commerce, and to do all other acts and things which independent states may of right do."

They further solemnly declared that whenever any "form of government becomes destructive of the ends for which it was established, it is the right of the people to alter or abolish it, and to institute a new government." Deeming the government of Great Britain to have become destructive of these ends, they declared that the colonies "are absolved from all allegiance to the British Crown, and that all political connection between them and the state of Great Britain is, and ought to be, totally dissolved."

In pursuance of this Declaration of Independence, each of the thirteen states proceeded to exercise its separate sovereignty; adopted for itself a constitution, and appointed officers for the administration of government in all its departments—legislative, executive, and judicial. For purposes of defense they united their arms and their counsels; and, in 1778, they entered into a league known as the Articles of Confederation, whereby they agreed to entrust the administration of their external relations to a common agent, known as the Congress of the United States, expressly declaring, in the first article, "that each state retains its sovereignty, freedom, and independence, and every power, jurisdiction, and right which is not, by this Confederation, expressly delegated to the United States in Congress assembled."

Under this Confederation, the War of the Revolution was carried on; and on the third of September 1783, the contest ended, and a definite treaty was signed by Great Britain, in which she acknowledged the independence of the colonies. . . . Thus were established the two great principles asserted by the colonies, namely, the right of a state to govern itself; and the right of a people to abolish a government when it becomes destructive of the ends for which it was instituted. And concurrent with the establishment of these principles was the fact that each colony became and was recognized by the mother country as a *free, sovereign, and independent state.*

In 1787, deputies were appointed by the states to revise the Articles of Confederation; and on seventeenth September 1787, these deputies recommended, for the adoption of the states, the articles of union, known as the Constitution of the United States. . . . By this Constitution, certain duties were imposed upon the several states, and the exercise of certain of their powers was restrained, which necessarily impelled their continued existence as sovereign states. But, to remove all doubt, an amendment was added, which declared that the powers not delegated to the United States by the Constitution, nor prohibited by it to the states, are reserved to the states respectively, or to the people. On the twenty-third May 1788, South Carolina, by a convention of her people, passed an ordinance assenting to this Constitution and afterward altered her own constitution to conform herself to the obligations she had undertaken.

Thus was established, by compact between the states, a government with defined objects and powers, limited to the express words of the grant. This limitation left the whole remaining mass of power subject to the clause reserving it to the states or the people, and rendered unnecessary any specification of reserved rights. We hold that the government thus established is subject to the two great principles asserted in the Declaration of Independence; and we hold further, that the mode of its formation subjects it to a third fundamental principle, namely, the law of compact. We maintain that in every compact between two or more parties, the obligation is mutual; that the failure of one of the contracting parties to perform a material part of the agreement entirely releases the obligation of the other; and that, where no arbiter is provided, each party is remitted to his own judgment to determine the fact of failure, with all its consequences.

In the present case that fact is established with certainty. We assert that fourteen of the states have deliberately refused for years past to fulfill their constitutional obligations, and we refer to their own statutes for the proof.

The Constitution of the United States, in its fourth article, provides as follows:

"No person held to service or labor in one state, under the laws thereof, escaping into another, shall, in consequence of any law or regulation therein, be discharged from such service or labor, but shall be delivered up on claim of the party to whom such service or labor may be due."

This stipulation was so material to the compact that without it that compact would not have been made. The greater number of the contracting parties held slaves, and they had previously evinced their estimate of the value of such a stipulation by making it a condition in the ordinance for the government of the territory ceded by Virginia, which obligations, and the laws of the general government, have ceased to effect the objects of the Constitution. The states of Maine, New Hampshire, Vermont, Massachusetts, Connecticut, Rhode Island, New York, Pennsylvania, Illinois, Indiana, Michigan, Wisconsin, and Iowa have enacted laws which either nullify the acts of Congress, or render useless any attempt to execute them.

The ends for which this Constitution was framed are declared by itself to be "to form a more perfect union, to establish justice, insure domestic tranquillity, provide for the common defense, promote the general welfare, and secure the blessings of liberty to ourselves and our posterity. . . ."

We affirm that these ends for which this government was instituted have been defeated, and the government itself has been destructive of them by the action of the nonslaveholding states. Those states have assumed the right of deciding upon the propriety of our domestic institutions; and have denied the rights of property established in fifteen of the states and recognized by the Constitution; they have denounced as sinful the institution of slavery; they have permitted the open establishment among them of societies whose avowed object is to disturb the peace of and eloign the property of the citizens of other states. They have encouraged and assisted thousands of our slaves to leave their homes; and those who remain have been incited by emissaries, books, and pictures to servile insurrection.

For twenty-five years this agitation has been steadily increasing until now it has secured to its aid the power of the common government. Observing the forms of the Constitution, a sectional party has found within that article establishing the executive department the means of subverting the Constitution itself. A geographical line has been drawn across the Union, and all the states north of that line have united in the election of a man to the high office of president of the United States, whose opinions and purposes are hostile to slavery. He is to be entrusted with the administration of the common government because he has declared that that "government cannot endure permanently half slave, half free" and that the public mind must rest in the belief that slavery is in the course of ultimate extinction. This sectional combination for the subversion of the Constitution has been aided, in some of the states, by elevating to citizenship persons who, by the supreme law of the land, are incapable of becoming citizens; and their votes have been used to inaugurate a new policy, hostile to the South and destructive of its peace and safety.

On the fourth of March next this party will take possession of the government. It has announced that the South shall be excluded from the common territory, and that the judicial tribunal shall be made sectional, and that a war must be waged against slavery until it shall cease throughout the United States.

The guarantees of the Constitution will then no longer exist; the equal rights of the states will be lost. The slaveholding states will no longer have the power of self-government, or self-protection, and the federal government will have become their enemy.

Sectional interest and animosity will deepen the irritation; and all hope of remedy is rendered vain by the fact that the public opinion at the North has invested a great political error with the sanctions of a more erroneous religious belief.

We, therefore, the people of South Carolina, by our delegates in convention assembled, appealing to the Supreme Judge of the world for the rectitude of our intentions, have solemnly declared that the Union heretofore existing between this state and the other states of North America is dissolved, and that the state of South Carolina has resumed her position among the nations of the world, as separate and independent state, with full power to levy war, conclude peace, contract alliances, establish commerce, and to do all other acts and things which independent states may of right do.

Battle Hymn of the Republic

Mine eyes have seen the glory of the coming of the Lord:
He is tramping out the vintage where the grapes of wrath are
    stored;
He hath loosed the fateful lightning of his terrible swift
    sword:
  His truth is marching on.

I have seen him in the watch-fires of a hundred circling
    camps;
They have builded him an altar in the evening dews and
    damps;
I can read his righteous sentence by the dim and flaring
    lamps:
  His day is marching on.

I have read a fiery gospel, writ in burnished rows of steel:
"As ye deal with my contemners, so with you my grace shall
    deal;
Let the hero, born of woman, crush the serpent with his heel,
  Since God is marching on."

He has sounded forth the trumpet that shall never call
    retreat;
He is sifting out the hearts of men before his judgment seat:
O, be swift, my soul, to answer him! be jubilant, my feet!
  Our God is marching on.

In the beauty of the lilies Christ was born across the sea,
With the glory in his bosom that transfigures you and me;
As he died to make men holy, let us die to make men free,
  While God is marching on.

JULIA WARD HOWE

SHILOH: A REQUIEM

April 1862

Skimming lightly, wheeling still,
   The swallows fly low
Over the fields in clouded days,
   The forest-field of Shiloh—
Over the field where April rain
Solaced the parched one stretched in pain
Through the pause of night
That followed the Sunday fight
   Around the church of Shiloh—
The church so lone, the log-built one,
That echoed to many a parting groan
     And natural prayer
   Of dying foemen mingled there—
Foemen at morn, but friends at eve—
   Fame or country least their care:
(What like a bullet can undeceive!)
   But now they lie low,
While over them the swallows skim,
   And all is hushed at Shiloh.

HERMAN MELVILLE

The Emancipation Proclamation

January 1, 1863

Whereas, On the twenty-second day of September, in the year of Our Lord one thousand eight hundred and sixty-two, a proclamation was issued by the president of the United States, containing, among other things, the following, to wit:

"That on the first day of January, in the year of Our Lord one thousand eight hundred and sixty-three, all persons held as slaves within any state, or designated part of a state, the people whereof shall then be in rebellion against the United States, shall be then, thenceforward, and forever free; and the executive government of the United States, including the military and naval authority thereof, will recognize and maintain the freedom of such persons, and will do no act or acts to repress such persons, or any of them, in any efforts they may make for their actual freedom.

"That the executive will, on the first day of January aforesaid, by proclamation, designate the states and parts of states, if any, in which the people thereof respectively shall then be in rebellion against the United States; and the fact that any state, or the people thereof, shall on that day be in good faith represented in the Congress of the United States by members chosen thereto at elections wherein a majority of the qualified voters of such state shall have participated, shall in the absence of strong countervailing testimony be deemed conclusive evidence that such state and the people thereof are not then in rebellion against the United States."

Now, therefore, I, Abraham Lincoln, president of the United States, by virtue of the power in me vested as commander in chief of the army and navy of the United States, in time of actual armed rebellion against the authority and government of the United States, and as a fit and necessary war measure for suppressing said rebellion, do, on this first day of January, in the year of Our Lord one thousand eight hundred and sixty-three, and in accordance with my purpose so to do, publicly proclaimed for the full period of one hundred days from the day first above mentioned, order and designate as the states and parts of states wherein the people thereof, respectively, are this day in rebellion against the United States, the following, to wit:

Arkansas, Texas, Louisiana (except the parishes of St. Bernard, Plaquemines, Jefferson, St. John, St. Charles, St. James, Ascension, Assumption, Terre Bonne, Lafourche, St. Mary, St. Martin, and Orleans, including the city of New Orleans), Mississippi, Alabama, Florida, Georgia, South Carolina, North Carolina, and Virginia (except the forty-eight counties designated as West Virginia, and also the counties of Berkeley, Accomac, Northampton, Elizabeth City, York, Princess Ann, and Norfolk, including the cities of Norfolk and Portsmouth), and which excepted parts are for the present left precisely as if this proclamation were not issued.

And by virtue of the power and for the purpose aforesaid, I do order and declare that all persons held as slaves within said designated states and parts of states are, and henceforward shall be, free; and that the executive government of the United States, including the military and naval authorities thereof, will recognize and maintain the freedom of said persons.

And I hereby enjoin upon the people so declared to be free to abstain from all violence, unless in necessary self-defense; and I recommend to them that, in all cases when allowed, they labor faithfully for reasonable wages.

And I further declare and make known that such persons of suitable condition will be received into the armed service of the United States to garrison forts, positions, stations, and other places, and to man vessels of all sorts in said service.

And upon this act, sincerely believed to be an act of justice, warranted by the Constitution upon military necessity, I invoke the considerate judgment of mankind and the gracious favor of Almighty God.

In witness whereof, I have hereunto set my hand, and caused the seal of the United States to be affixed.

Done at the city of Washington, this first day of January, in the year of Our Lord one thousand eight hundred and sixty-three, and of the independence of the United States of America the eighty-seventh.

PRESIDENT ABRAHAM LINCOLN

BARBARA FRIETCHIE

Up from the meadows rich with corn,
Clear in the cool September morn,

The clustered spires of Frederick stand
Green-walled by the hills of Maryland.

Round about them orchards sweep,
Apple and peach tree fruited deep,

Fair as the garden of the Lord
To the eyes of the famished rebel horde,

On that pleasant morn of the early fall
When Lee marched over the mountain-wall;

Over the mountains winding down,
Horse and foot, into Frederick town.

Forty flags with their silver stars,
Forty flags with their crimson bars,

Flapped in the morning wind: the sun
Of noon looked down, and saw not one.

Up rose old Barbara Frietchie then,
Bowed with her fourscore years and ten;

Bravest of all in Frederick town,
She took up the flag the men hauled down;

In her attic window the staff she set,
To show that one heart was loyal yet.

Up the street came the rebel tread,
Stonewall Jackson riding ahead.

Under his slouched hat left and right
He glanced; the old flag met his sight.

"Halt!"—the dust-brown ranks stood fast.
"Fire!"—out blazed the rifle-blast.

It shivered the window, pane and sash;
It rent the banner with seam and gash.

Quick, as it fell, from the broken staff
Dame Barbara snatched the silken scarf.

She leaned far out on the windowsill,
And shook it forth with a royal will.

"Shoot, if you must, this old gray head,
But spare your country's flag," she said.

A shade of sadness, a blush of shame,
Over the face of the leader came;

The nobler nature within him stirred
To life at that woman's deed and word;

"Who touches a hair of yon gray head
Dies like a dog! March on!" he said.

All day long through Frederick street
Sounded the tread of marching feet:

All day long that free flag tost
Over the heads of the rebel host.

Ever its torn folds rose and fell
On the loyal winds that loved it well;

And through the hill-gaps sunset light
Shone over it with a warm good night.

Barbara Frietchie's work is o'er,
And the rebel rides on his raids no more.

Honor to her! and let a tear
Fall, for her sake, on Stonewall's bier.

Over Barbara Frietchie's grave,
Flag of freedom and union, wave!

Peace and order and beauty draw
Round thy symbol of light and law;

And ever the stars above look down
On thy stars below in Frederick town!

JOHN GREENLEAF WHITTIER

CHARLESTON

April 1863

Calm as that second summer which precedes
The first fall of the snow,
In the broad sunlight of heroic deeds,
The city bides the foe.

As yet, behind their ramparts, stern and proud,
Her bolted thunders sleep—
Dark Sumter, like a battlemented cloud,
Looms o'er the solemn deep.

No Calpe frowns from lofty cliff or scaur
To guard the holy strand;
But Moultrie holds in leash her dogs of war
Above the level sand.

And down the dunes a thousand guns lie couched,
Unseen, beside the flood—
Like tigers in some Orient jungle crouched,
That wait and watch for blood.

Meanwhile, through streets still echoing with trade,
Walk grave and thoughtful men,
Whose hands may one day wield the patriot's blade
As lightly as the pen.

And maidens, with such eyes as would grow dim
Over a bleeding hound,
Seem each one to have caught the strength of him
Whose sword she sadly bound.

Thus girt without and garrisoned at home,
Day patient following day,

Old Charleston looks from roof and spire and dome,
Across her tranquil bay.

Ships, through a hundred foes, from Saxon lands
And spicy Indian ports,
Bring Saxon steel and iron to her hands,
And summer to her courts.

But still, along yon dim Atlantic line,
The only hostile smoke
Creeps like a harmless mist above the brine,
From some frail floating oak.

Shall the spring dawn, and she, still clad in smiles,
And with an unscathed brow,
Rest in the strong arms of her palm-crowned isles,
As fair and free as now?

We know not; in the temple of the Fates
God has inscribed her doom:
And, all untroubled in her faith, she waits
The triumph or the tomb.

HENRY TIMROD

JOHN BURNS OF GETTYSBURG

July 1–3, 1863

Have you heard the story that gossips tell
Of Burns of Gettysburg? No? Ah, well:
Brief is the glory that hero earns,
Briefer the story of poor John Burns:
He was the fellow who won renown—
The only man who didn't back down
When the rebels rode through his native town;
But held his own in the fight next day,
When all his townsfolk ran away.
That was in July, sixty-three—
The very day that General Lee,
Flower of Southern chivalry,
Baffled and beaten, backward reeled
From a stubborn Meade and a barren field.

I might tell how, but the day before,
John Burns stood at his cottage door,
Looking down the village street,
Where, in the shade of his peaceful vine,
He heard the low of his gathered kine,
And felt their breath with incense sweet;
Or I might say, when the sunset burned
The old farm gable, he thought it turned
The milk that fell like a babbling flood
Into the milk-pail, red as blood!
Or how he fancied the hum of bees
Were bullets buzzing among the trees.
But all such fanciful thoughts as these
Were strange to a practical man like Burns,
Who minded only his own concerns,
Troubled no more by fancies fine
Than one of his calm-eyed, long-tailed kine—

Quite old-fashioned and matter-of-fact,
Slow to argue, but quick to act.
That was the reason, as some folks say,
He fought so well on that terrible day.
And it was terrible. On the right
Raged for hours the heady fight,
Thundered the battery's double bass—
Difficult music for men to face;
While on the left—where now the graves
Undulate like the living waves
That all that day unceasing swept
Up to the pits the rebels kept—
Round-shot ploughed the upland glades,
Sown with bullets, reaped with blades;
Shattered fences here and there
Tossed their splinters in the air;
The very trees were stripped and bare;
The barns that once held yellow grain
Were heaped with harvests of the slain;
The cattle bellowed on the plain,
The turkeys screamed with might and main,
The brooding barn-fowl left their rest
With strange shells bursting in each nest.

Just where the tide of battle turns,
Erect and lonely, stood old John Burns.
How do you think the man was dressed?
He wore an ancient long buff vest,
Yellow as saffron—but his best;
And, buttoned over his manly breast,
Was a bright blue coat, with a rolling collar,
And large gilt buttons—size of a dollar—
With tails that the country-folk called "swaller."
He wore a broad-brimmed, bell-crowned hat,
White as the locks on which it sat.

Never had such a sight been seen
For forty years on the village green,
Since old John Burns was a country beau,
And went to the "quiltings" long ago.

Close at his elbows all that day,
Veterans of the Peninsula,
Sunburnt and bearded, charged away;
And striplings, downy of lip and chin—
Clerks that the Home-Guard mustered in—
Glanced, as they passed, at the hat he wore,
Then at the rifle his right hand bore;
And hailed him, from out their youthful lore,
With scraps of a slangy repertoire:
"How are you, White Hat?" "Put her through!"
"Your head's level!" and "Bully for you!"
Called him "Daddy"—begged he'd disclose
The name of the tailor who made his clothes,
And what was the value he set on those;
While Burns, unmindful of jeer or scoff,
Stood there picking the rebels off—
With his long brown rifle, and bell-crowned hat,
And the swallow-tails they were laughing at.

'Twas but a moment, for that respect
Which clothes all courage their voices checked;
And something the wildest could understand
Spake in the old man's strong right hand,
And his corded throat, and the lurking frown
Of his eyebrows under his old bell-crown;
Until, as they gazed, there crept an awe
Through the ranks in whispers, and some men saw,
In the antique vestments and long white hair,
The past of the nation in battle there;
And some of the soldiers since declare

That the gleam of his old white hat afar,
Like the crested plume of the brave Navarre,
That day was their oriflamme of war.

So raged the battle. You know the rest:
How the rebels, beaten and backward pressed,
Broke at the final charge and ran.
At which John Burns—a practical man—
Shouldered his rifle, unbent his brows,
And then went back to his bees and cows.
That is the story of old John Burns;
This is the moral the reader learns:
In fighting the battle, the question's whether
You'll show a hat that's white, or a feather!

BRET HARTE

SHERIDAN'S RIDE

October 19, 1864

Up from the South at break of day,
Bringing to Winchester fresh dismay,
The affrighted air with a shudder bore,
Like a herald in haste, to the chieftain's door,
The terrible grumble and rumble and roar,
Telling the battle was on once more,
And Sheridan twenty miles away.

And wider still those billows of war
Thundered along the horizon's bar,
And louder yet into Winchester rolled
The roar of that red sea uncontrolled,
Making the blood of the listener cold
As he thought of the stake in that fiery fray,
With Sheridan twenty miles away.

But there is a road from Winchester town,
A good, broad highway leading down;
And there through the flash of the morning light,
A steed as black as the steeds of night,
Was seen to pass as with eagle flight.
As if he knew the terrible need,
He stretched away with the utmost speed;
Hills rose and fell—but his heart was gay,
With Sheridan fifteen miles away.

Under his spurning feet the road
Like an arrowy alpine river flowed,
And the landscape sped away behind
Like an ocean flying before the wind;
And the steed, like a bark fed with furnace ire,
Swept on with his wild eyes full of fire;

But, lo! he is nearing his heart's desire,
He is snuffing the smoke of the roaring fray,
With Sheridan only five miles away.

The first that the general saw were the groups
Of stragglers, and then the retreating troops;
What was done—what to do—a glance told him both,
And, striking his spurs with a terrible oath,
He dashed down the line mid a storm of huzzas,
And the wave of retreat checked its course there because
The sight of the master compelled it to pause.
With foam and with dust the black charger was gray,
By the flash of his eye, and his nostril's play
He seemed to the whole great army to say,
"I have brought you Sheridan all the way
From Winchester, down to save the day!"
Hurrah, hurrah for Sheridan!
Hurrah, hurrah for horse and man!
And when their statues are placed on high.
Under the dome of the Union sky—
The American soldier's Temple of Fame—
There with the glorious general's name
Be it said in letters both bold and bright:
"Here is the steed that saved the day
By carrying Sheridan into the fight,
From Winchester—twenty miles away!"

THOMAS BUCHANAN READ

From Sojourner Truth to Rowland Johnson: On Her Visit to President Abraham Lincoln

Freedman's Village, Va., Nov. 17, 1864

Dear Friend:

I am at Freedman's Village. After visiting the president. I spent three weeks at Mrs. Swisshelm's, and held two meetings in Washington, at Rev. Mr. Garnet's Presbyterian Church, for the benefit of the Colored Soldiers' Aid Society. These meetings were successful in raising funds. One week after that I went to Mason's Island, and saw the freedmen there, and held several meetings, remained a week and was present at the celebration of the emancipation of the slaves of Maryland, and spoke on that occasion.

It was about 8 o'clock A.M., when I called on the president. Upon entering his reception room we found about a dozen persons in waiting, among them two colored women. I had quite a pleasant time waiting until he was disengaged, and enjoyed his conversation with others; he showed as much kindness and consideration to the colored persons as to the whites—if there was any difference, more. One case was that of a colored woman who was sick and likely to be turned out of her house on account of her inability to pay her rent. The president listened to her with much attention, and spoke to her with kindness and tenderness. He said he had given so much he could give no more, but told her where to go and get the money, and asked Mrs. C———n to assist her, which she did.

The president was seated at his desk. Mrs. C. said to him, "This is Sojourner Truth, who has come all the way from Michigan to see you." He then arose, gave me his hand, made a bow, and said, "I am pleased to see you."

I said to him, Mr. President, when you first took your seat

I feared you would be torn to pieces, for I likened you unto Daniel, who was thrown into the lion's den; and if the lions did not tear you into pieces, I knew that it would be God that had saved you; and I said if he spared me I would see you before the four years expired, and he has done so, and now I am here to see you for myself.

He then congratulated me on my having been spared. Then I said, I appreciate you, for you are the best president who has ever taken the seat. He replied: "I expect you have reference to my having emancipated the slaves in my proclamation. But," said he, mentioning the names of several of his predecessors (and among them emphatically that of Washington), "they were all just as good, and would have done just as I have done if the time had come. If the people over the river [pointing across the Potomac] had behaved themselves, I could not have done what I have; but they did not, which gave me the opportunity to do these things." I then said, I thank God that you were the instrument selected by him and the people to do it. I told him that I had never heard of him before he was talked of for president. He smilingly replied, "I had heard of you many times before that."

He then showed me the Bible presented to him by the colored people of Baltimore, of which you have no doubt seen a description. I have seen it for myself, and it is beautiful beyond description. After I had looked it over, I said to him, This is beautiful indeed; the colored people have given this to the head of the government, and that government once sanctioned laws that would not permit its people to learn enough to enable them to read this book. And for what? Let them answer who can.

I must say, and I am proud to say, that I never was treated by anyone with more kindness and cordiality than were shown to me by that great and good man, Abraham Lincoln, by the grace of God president of the United States for four years more. He took my little book, and with the same hand that signed the death warrant of slavery, he wrote as follows:

"For Aunty Sojourner Truth, Oct. 29, 1864. A. Lincoln."

As I was taking my leave, he arose and took my hand, and

said he would be pleased to have me call again. I felt that I was in the presence of a friend, and I now thank God from the bottom of my heart that I always have advocated his cause, and have done it openly and boldly. I shall feel still more in duty bound to do so in time to come. May God assist me.

Now I must tell you something of this place. I found things quite as well as I expected. I think I can be useful and will stay. The captain in command of the guard has given me his assistance, and by his aid I have obtained a little house, and will move into it tomorrow. Will you ask Mrs. P., or any of my friends, to send me a couple of sheets and a pillow? I find many of the women very ignorant in relation to housekeeping, as most of them were instructed in field labor, but not in household duties. They all seem to think a great deal of me, and want to learn the way we live in the North. I am listened to with attention and respect, and from all things, I judge it is the will of both God and the people that I should remain.

Now when you come to Washington, don't forget to call and see me. You may publish my whereabouts, and anything in this letter you think would interest the friends of freedom, justice, and truth, in the *Standard* and *Anglo-African,* and any other paper you may see fit.

Enclosed please find four shadows [cartes de visite]. The two dollars came safely. Anything in the way of nourishment you may feel like sending, send it along. The captain sends to Washington every day. Give my love to all who inquire for me, and tell my friends to direct all things for me to the care of Capt. George B. Carse, Freedman's Village, Va. Ask Mr. Oliver Johnson to please send me the *Standard* while I am here, as many of the colored people like to hear what is going on, and to know what is being done for them. Sammy, my grandson, reads for them. We are both well, and happy, and feel that we are in good employment. I find plenty of friends.

Your friend,
SOJOURNER TRUTH
From *Narrative of Sojourner Truth,* 1878

Second Inaugural Address of President Abraham Lincoln

March 4, 1865

Fellow Countrymen: At this second appearing to take the oath of the presidential office, there is less occasion for an extended address than there was at the first. Then a statement, somewhat in detail, of a course to be pursued, seemed fitting and proper. Now, at the expiration of four years, during which public declarations have been constantly called forth on every point and phase of the great contest which still absorbs the attention and engrosses the energies of the nation, little that is new could be presented. The progress of our arms, upon which all else chiefly depends, is as well known to the public as to myself; and it is, I trust, reasonably satisfactory and encouraging to all. With high hope for the future, no prediction in regard to it is ventured.

On the occasion corresponding to this four years ago, all thoughts were anxiously directed to an impending civil war. All dreaded it—all sought to avert it. While the inaugural address was being delivered from this place, devoted altogether to saving the Union without war, insurgent agents were in the city seeking to destroy it without war—seeking to dissolve the Union, and divide effects, by negotiation. Both parties deprecated war; but one of them would make war rather than let the nation survive; and the other would accept war rather than let it perish. And the war came.

One-eighth of the whole population were colored slaves, not distributed generally over the Union, but localized in the southern part of it. These slaves constituted a peculiar and powerful interest. All knew that this interest was, somehow, the cause of the war. To strengthen, perpetuate, and extend this interest was the object for which the insurgents would rend the Union, even by war; while the government claimed no right to do more than to restrict the territorial enlargement of it. Neither party expected for the war, the magnitude, or the duration, which it has already attained. Neither anticipated that the cause of the conflict might cease with, or even before, the conflict itself should cease. Each looked for an easier triumph, and a result less fundamental and astounding.

Both read the same Bible, and pray to the same God; and each invokes His aid against the other. It may seem strange that any men should dare to ask a just God's assistance in wringing their bread from the sweat of other men's faces; but let us judge not that we be not judged. The prayers of both could not be answered; that of neither has been answered fully.

The Almighty has His own purposes. "Woe unto the world because of offenses! For it must needs be that offenses come; but woe to that man by whom the offense cometh!" If we shall suppose that American slavery is one of those offenses which, in the providence of God, must needs come, but which, having continued through His appointed time, He now wills to remove, and that He gives to both North and South, this terrible war, as the woe due to those by whom the offense came, shall we discern therein any departure from those divine attributes which the believers in a living God always ascribe to Him? Fondly do we hope—fervently do we pray—that this mighty scourge of war may speedily pass away. Yet, if God wills that it continue, until all the wealth piled by the bondman's 250 years of unrequited toil shall be sunk, and until every drop of blood drawn with the lash, shall be paid by another drawn with the sword, as was said three thousand years ago, so still it must be said "the judgments of the Lord are true and righteous altogether."

With malice toward none, with charity for all; with firmness in the right, as God gives us to see the right, let us strive on to finish the work we are in; to bind up the nation's wounds; to care for him who shall have borne the battle, and for his widow, and his orphan—to do all which may achieve and cherish a just, and a lasting peace, among ourselves, and with all nations.

General Robert E. Lee's Farewell Letter to His Army

Hd. Qrs. A. N. Va., 10 April 1865,
Gen'l Order No. 9

After four years of arduous service marked by unsurpassed courage and fortitude, the Army of Northern Virginia has been compelled to yield to overwhelming numbers and resources.

I need not tell the brave survivors of so many hard fought battles, who have remained steadfast to the last, that I have consented to this result from no distrust of them; but feeling that valor and devotion could accomplish nothing that could compensate for the loss that must have attended the continuance of the contest, I determined to avoid the useless sacrifice of those whose past services have endeared them to their countrymen.

By the terms of the agreement, officers and men can return to their homes and remain until exchanged. You will take with you the satisfaction that proceeds from the consciousness of duty faithfully performed; and I earnestly pray that a Merciful God will extend to you His blessing and protection.

With an unceasing admiration of your constancy and devotion to your country, and a grateful remembrance of your kind and generous consideration for myself, I bid you all an affectionate farewell.

R. E. Lee,
Gen'l.

O Captain! My Captain!

O Captain! my Captain! our fearful trip is done,
The ship has weather'd every rack, the prize we sought is
    won.
  The port is near, the bells I hear, the people all exulting,
  While follow eyes the steady keel, the vessel grim and
    daring;

        But O heart! heart! heart!
          O the bleeding drops of red,
        Where on the deck my Captain lies,
          Fallen cold and dead.

O Captain! my Captain! rise up and hear the bells;
Rise up—for you the flag is flung—for you the bugle trills,
  For you bouquets and ribbon'd wreaths—for you the
    shores a-crowding,
  For you they call, the swaying mass, their eager faces
    turning;

        Here, Captain! dear father!
          This arm beneath your head!
        It is some dream that on the deck,
          You've fallen cold and dead.

My Captain does not answer, his lips are pale and still,
My father does not feel my arm, he has no pulse nor will,
  The ship is anchor'd safe and sound, its voyage closed and
    done,
  From fearful trip the victor ship comes in with object won;

        Exult, O shores! and ring, O bells!
          But I with mournful tread,
        Walk the deck my Captain lies,
          Fallen cold and dead.

WALT WHITMAN

THE BLUE AND THE GRAY

By the flow of the inland river,
   Whence the fleets of iron have fled,
Where the blades of the grave-grass quiver,
   Asleep on the ranks of the dead;
     Under the sod and the dew,
       Waiting the judgment day;
     Under the one, the Blue;
       Under the other, the Gray.

These in the robings of glory,
   Those in the gloom of defeat;
All with the battle-blood gory,
   In the dusk of eternity meet;
     Under the sod and the dew,
       Waiting the judgment day;
     Under the laurel, the Blue;
       Under the willow, the Gray.

From the silence of sorrowful hours,
   The desolate mourners go,
Lovingly laden with flowers,
   Alike for the friend and the foe;
     Under the sod and the dew,
       Waiting the judgment day;
     Under the roses, the Blue;
       Under the lilies, the Gray.

So, with an equal splendor,
   The morning sun-rays fall,
With a touch impartially tender,
   On the blossoms blooming for all;
     Under the sod and the dew,
       Waiting the judgment day;

Broidered with gold, the Blue;
  Mellowed with gold, the Gray.

So, when the summer calleth,
  On forest and field of grain,
With an equal murmur falleth
  The cooling drip of the rain;
    Under the sod and the dew,
      Waiting the judgment day;
    Wet with the rain, the Blue;
      Wet with the rain, the Gray.

Sadly, but not with upbraiding,
  The generous deed was done;
In the storm of the years that are fading,
  No braver battle was won;
    Under the sod and the dew,
      Waiting the judgment day;
    Under the blossoms, the Blue;
      Under the garlands, the Gray.

No more shall the war-cry sever,
  Or the winding rivers be red;
They banish our anger for ever,
  When they laurel the graves of our dead.
    Under the sod and the dew,
      Waiting the judgment day;
    Love and tears for the Blue;
      Tears and love for the Gray.

FRANCIS MILES FINCH

LINCOLN

Hurt was the nation with a mighty wound,
And all her ways were filled with clam'rous sound.
Wailed loud the South with unremitting grief,
And wept the North that could not find relief.
Then madness joined its harshest tone to strife:
A minor note swelled in the song of life
Till, stirring with the love that filled his breast,
But still, unflinching at the right's behest
Grave Lincoln came, strong-handed, from afar—
The mighty Homer of the lyre of war!
'Twas he who bade the raging tempest cease,
Wrenched from his strings the harmony of peace,
Muted the strings that made the discord—wrong,
And gave his spirit up in thund'rous song.
Oh, mighty master of the mighty lyre!
Earth heard and trembled at, thy strains of fire:
Earth learned of thee what heav'n already knew,
And wrote thee down among her treasured few!

PAUL LAURENCE DUNBAR

ABRAHAM LINCOLN WALKS
AT MIDNIGHT

It is portentous, and a thing of state
    That here at midnight, in our little town
A mourning figure walks, and will not rest
    Near the old courthouse pacing up and down.

Or by his homestead, or the shadowed yards
  He lingers where his children used to play,
Or through the market, on the well-worn stones
  He stalks until the dawn-stars burn away.

A bronzed, lank man! His suit of ancient black,
  A famous high top hat and plain worn shawl
Make him the quaint great figure that men love,
  The prairie lawyer, master of us all.

He cannot sleep upon his hillside now.
  He is among us, as in times before!
And we who toss and lie awake for long
  Breathe deep, and start, to see him pass the door.

His head is bowed. He thinks on men and kings.
  Yea, when the sick world cries, how can he sleep?
Too many peasants fight, they know not why,
  Too many homesteads in black terror weep.

The sins of all the warlords burn his heart.
  He sees the dreadnaughts scouring every main.
He carries on his shawl-wrapt shoulders now
  The bitterness, the folly and the pain.

He cannot rest until a spirit-dawn
  Shall come—the shining hope of Europe free;
The league of sober folk, the Workers' Earth
  Bringing long peace to cornland, alp, and sea.

It breaks his heart that kings must murder still,
  That all his hours of travail here for men
Seem yet in vain. And who will bring white peace
  That he may sleep upon his hill again?

VACHEL LINDSAY

PART THREE

——— ★ ———

All Across the Land

ALTHOUGH THE UNITED STATES began its independent existence as a republic of thirteen states on the eastern coast of the continent, the leaders of the nation always believed that its destiny lay in westward expansion. President Thomas Jefferson negotiated the purchase of the Louisiana Territory from France in 1803 and within a year sent Meriwether Lewis and William Clark to explore the land west of the Mississippi. In 1823, President James Monroe, influenced by his secretary of state, John Quincy Adams, promulgated the famous Monroe Doctrine, warning European nations not to interfere in the affairs of the Western Hemisphere.

In the course of the movement westward, Texas became first an independent republic, with Sam Houston as its president, and then a state. President James K. Polk, who promoted war with Mexico, firmly believed in western expansion, and the territories of Utah, Nevada, New Mexico, California, and Oregon were acquired by the end of his administration in 1848, thus stretching the nation from the Atlantic to the Pacific.

This pioneering spirit, as well as the unique character of America's diverse regions and cities and its magnificent landscape, inspired celebratory essays by such writers as Henry David Thoreau, Sidney Lanier, and the naturalist John Muir, and paeans by many poets, including John Greenleaf Whittier, Joaquin Miller, Walt Whitman, Julia Ward Howe, Edmund Clarence Stedman, and Carl Sandburg.

From President Thomas Jefferson to Meriwether Lewis: On an Expedition to Land West of the Mississippi River

Washington, U.S. of America, July 4, 1803

Dear Sir:

In the journey which you are about to undertake for the discovery of the course and source of the Missouri, and of the most convenient water communication from thence to the Pacific ocean, your party being small, it is to be expected that you will encounter considerable dangers from the Indian inhabitants. should you escape those dangers and reach the Pacific ocean, you may find it imprudent to hazard a return the same way, and be forced to seek a passage round by sea, in such vessels as you may find on the Western coast. but you will be without money, without clothes, & other necessaries; as a sufficient supply cannot be carried with you from hence. your resource in that case can only be in the credit of the U. S. for which purpose I hereby authorise you to draw on the Secretaries of State, of the Treasury, of War & of the Navy of the U. S. according as you may find your draughts will be most negociable, for the purpose of obtaining money or necessaries for yourself & your men; and I solemnly pledge the faith of the United States that these draughts shall be paid punctually at the date they are made payable. I also ask of the Consuls, agents, merchants & citizens of any nation with which we have intercourse or amity to furnish you with those supplies which your necessities may call for, assuring them of honorable and prompt retribution. and our own Consuls in foreign parts where you may happen to be, are hereby instructed & required to be aiding & assisting you in whatsoever may be necessary for procuring your return back to the United States. And to give more entire satisfaction & confidence to those who may be disposed to aid you, I Thomas Jefferson, President of the United States of America, have written this letter of general credit for you with my own hand, and signed it with my name.

TH: JEFFERSON
To Capt. Meriwether Lewis

THE MONROE DOCTRINE

December 2, 1823

At the proposal of the Russian Imperial government, made through the minister of the emperor residing here, a full power and instructions have been transmitted to the minister of the United States at St. Petersburg to arrange by amicable negotiation the respective rights and interests of the two nations on the northwest coast of this continent. A similar proposal had been made by His Imperial Majesty to the government of Great Britain, which has likewise been acceded to. The government of the United States has been desirous, by this friendly proceeding, of manifesting the great value which they have invariably attached to the friendship of the emperor and their solicitude to cultivate the best understanding with his government. In the discussions to which this interest has given rise and in the arrangements by which they may terminate, the occasion has been judged proper for asserting, as a principle in which the rights and interests of the United States are involved, that the American continents, by the free and independent condition which they have assumed and maintain, are henceforth not to be considered as subjects for future colonization by any European powers. . . .

It was stated at the commencement of the last session that a great effort was then making in Spain and Portugal to improve the condition of the people of those countries, and that it appeared to be conducted with extraordinary moderation. It need scarcely be remarked that the result has been so far very different from what was then anticipated.

Of events in that quarter of the globe, with which we have so much intercourse and from which we derive our origin, we have always been anxious and interested spectators. The citizens of the United States cherish sentiments the most friendly in favor of the liberty and happiness of their fellow men on that side of the Atlantic. In the wars of the European powers in matters relating to themselves we have never taken any part, nor does it comport with our policy so to do. It is only when our rights are invaded or seriously menaced that we resent injuries or make preparation for our defense.

With the movements in this hemisphere we are of necessity more immediately connected, and by causes which must be obvious to all enlightened and impartial observers. The political system of the allied powers is essentially different in this respect from that of America. This difference proceeds from that which exists in their respective governments; and to the defense of our own, which has been achieved by the loss of so much blood and treasure, and matured by the wisdom of their most enlightened citizens, and under which we have enjoyed unexampled felicity, this whole nation is devoted.

We owe it, therefore, to candor and to the amicable relations existing between the United States and those powers to declare that we should consider any attempt on their part to extend their system to any portion of this hemisphere as dangerous to our peace and safety. With the existing colonies or dependencies of any European power we have not interfered and shall not interfere. But with the governments who have declared their independence and maintained it, and whose independence we have, on great consideration and on just principles, acknowledged, we could not view any interposition for the purpose of oppressing them, or controlling in any other manner their destiny, by any European power in any other light than as the manifestation of an unfriendly disposition toward the United States. In the war between those new governments and Spain we declared our neutrality at the time of their recognition, and to this we have adhered, and shall continue to adhere, provided no change shall occur which, in the judgment of the competent authorities of this government, shall make a corresponding change on the part of the United States indispensable to their security.

The late events in Spain and Portugal show that Europe is still unsettled. Of this important fact no stronger proof can be adduced than that the allied powers should have thought it proper, on any principle satisfactory to themselves, to have interposed by force in the internal concerns of Spain. To what extent such interposition may be carried, on the same principle, is a question in which all independent powers whose governments differ from theirs are interested, even those most remote, and surely none more so than the United States. Our policy in regard to Europe, which was adopted at an early stage of the wars which have so long agitated that quarter of the globe, nevertheless remains the same, which is not to interfere in the internal concerns of any of its powers; to consider the government de facto as the legitimate government for us; to cultivate friendly relations with it, and to preserve those relations by a frank, firm, and manly policy, meeting in all instances the just claims of every power, submitting to injuries from none.

But in regard to those [American] continents circumstances are eminently and conspicuously different. It is impossible that the allied powers should extend their political system to any portion of either continent without endangering our peace and happiness; nor can anyone believe that our southern brethren, if left to themselves, would adopt it of their own accord. It is equally impossible, therefore, that we should behold such interposition in any form with indifference. If we look to the comparative strength and resources of Spain and those new governments, and their distance from each other, it must be obvious that she can never subdue them. It is still the true policy of the United States to leave the parties to themselves, in the hope that other powers will pursue the same course.

PRESIDENT JAMES MONROE

ON THE CONCORD AND MERRIMACK RIVERS

Sunday, September 1, 1839

As we glided over the broad bosom of the Merrimack, between Chelmsford and Dracut, at noon, here a quarter of a mile wide, the rattling of our oars was echoed over the water to those villages, and their slight sounds to us. Their harbors lay as smooth and fairylike as the Lido, or Syracuse, or Rhodes, in our imagination, while, like some strange roving craft, we flitted past what seemed the dwellings of noble home-staying men, seemingly as conspicuous as if on an eminence, or floating upon a tide which came up to those villagers' breasts. At a third of a mile over the water we heard distinctly some children repeating their catechism in a cottage near the shore, while in the broad shallows between, a herd of cows stood lashing their sides, and waging war with the flies. . . .

It was in fact an old battle and hunting ground through which we had been floating, the ancient dwelling-place of a race of hunters and warriors. Their weirs of stone, their arrowheads and hatchets, their pestles, and the mortars in which they pounded Indian corn before the white man had tasted it, lay concealed in the mud of the river bottom. Tradition still points out the spots where they took fish in the greatest numbers, by

such arts as they possessed. . . . Pawtucket and Wamesit, where
the Indians resorted in the fishing season, are now Lowell, the
city of spindles and Manchester of America, which sends its
cotton cloth round the globe. Even we youthful voyagers had
spent a part of our lives in the village of Chelmsford, when the
present city, whose bells we heard, was its obscure north district
only, and the giant weaver was not yet fairly born. So old are
we; so young is it.

We were thus entering the state of New Hampshire on the
bosom of the flood formed by the tribute of its innumerable
valleys. The river was the only key which could unlock its maze,
presenting its hills and valleys, its lakes and streams, in their
natural order and position. The Merrimack, or Sturgeon River,
is formed by the confluence of the Pemigewasset, which rises
near the Notch of the White Mountains, and the Winnipiseogee,
which drains the lake of the same name, signifying "The Smile
of the Great Spirit." From their junction it runs south seventy-
eight miles to Massachusetts, and thence east thirty-five miles to
the sea. I have traced its stream from where it bubbles out of the
rocks of the White Mountains above the clouds, to where it is
lost amid the salt billows of the ocean on Plum Island beach. At
first it comes on murmuring to itself by the base of stately and
retired mountains, through moist primitive woods whose juices
it receives, where the bear still drinks it, and the cabins of
settlers are far between, and there are few to cross its stream;
enjoying in solitude its cascades still unknown to fame; by long
ranges of mountains of Sandwich and of Squam, slumbering
like tumuli of Titans, with the peaks of Moosehillock, the Hay-
stack, and Kearsarge reflected in its waters; where the maple
and the raspberry, those lovers of the hills, flourish amid
temperate dews.

It was already the water of Squam and Newfound Lake and
Winnipiseogee, and White Mountain snow dissolved, on which
we were floating, and Smith's and Baker's and Mad rivers, and
Nashua and Souhegan and Piscataquoag, and Suncook and Sou-
cook and Contoocook, mingled in incalculable proportions, still

fluid, yellowish, restless all, with an ancient, ineradicable inclination to the sea.

So it flows on down by Lowell and Haverhill, at which last
place it first suffers a sea change, and a few masts betray the
vicinity of the ocean. Between the towns of Amesbury and
Newbury it is a broad commercial river, from a third to half a
mile in width, no longer skirted with yellow and crumbling
banks, but backed by high green hills and pastures, with frequent white beaches on which the fishermen draw up their nets.
I have passed down this portion of the river in a steamboat, and
it was a pleasant sight to watch from its deck the fishermen
dragging their seines on the distant shore, as in pictures of a
foreign strand. At intervals you may meet with a schooner laden
with lumber, standing up to Haverhill, or else lying at anchor
or aground, waiting for wind or tide; until, at last, you glide
under the famous Chain Bridge, and are landed at Newburyport. . . . From the steeples of Newburyport you may review this
river stretching far up into the country, with many a white sail
glancing over it like an inland sea, and behold, as one wrote who
was born on its head-waters, "Down out at its mouth, the dark
inky main blending with the blue above. Plum Island, its sand
ridges scolloping along the horizon like the sea serpent, and the
distant outline broken by many a tall ship, leaning still, against
the sky."

Rising at an equal height with the Connecticut, the
Merrimack reaches the sea by a course only half as long, and
hence has no leisure to form broad and fertile meadows, like the
former, but is hurried along rapids and down numerous falls,
without long delay. The banks are generally steep and high,
with a narrow interval reaching back to the hills, which is only
rarely or partially overflown at present, and is much valued by
the farmers. Between Chelmsford and Concord, in New Hampshire, it varies from twenty to seventy-five rods in width. It is
probably wider than it was formerly, in many places, owing to
the trees having been cut down and the consequent wasting
away of its banks. . . .

Unfitted to some extent for the purposes of commerce by the sandbar at its mouth, see how this river was devoted from the first to the service of manufactures. Issuing from the iron region of Franconia, and flowing through still uncut forests, by inexhaustible ledges of granite, Squam, and Winnipiseogee, and Newfound, and Massabesic lakes for its millponds, it falls over a succession of natural dams, where it has been offering its privileges in vain for ages, until at last the Yankee race came to improve them. Standing at its mouth, look up its sparkling stream to its source—a silver cascade which falls all the way from the White Mountains to the sea—and behold a city on each successive plateau, a busy colony of human beaver around every fall. Not to mention Newburyport and Haverhill, see Lawrence, and Lowell, and Nashua, and Manchester, and Concord, gleaming one above the other. When at length it has escaped from under the last of the factories, it has a level and unmolested passage to the sea, a mere waste water, as it were, bearing little with it but its fame; its pleasant course revealed by the morning fog which hangs over it, and the sails of the few small vessels which transact the commerce of Haverhill and Newburyport. But its real vessels are railroad cars, and its true and main stream, flowing by an iron channel farther south, may be traced by a long line of vapor amid the hills, which no morning wind ever disperses, to where it empties into the sea at Boston. This side is the louder murmur now. Instead of the scream of a fishhawk scaring the fishes, is heard the whistle of the steam engine, arousing a country to its progress.

HENRY DAVID THOREAU,
from *A Week on the Concord
and Merrimack Rivers,* 1849

FROM PRESIDENT SAM HOUSTON TO ANDREW JACKSON: ON THE ANNEXATION OF THE REPUBLIC OF TEXAS BY THE UNITED STATES

Washington, Texas, February 16, 1844

Venerated Friend,

Your several favors of the last month have reached me safely and with expedition. I have given all the attention to their contents which your views as well as the subject matter itself demanded. You are fully aware that every circumstance in which you feel a deep interest, or whatever concerns you individually, awakens in me emotions of the liveliest regard.

It is natural to suppose that the subject of the annexation of Texas to the U. States has commanded the most profound deliberation of which I am capable. Heretofore, the demeanor of the U. States towards us, has been such as to discourage any hope which the friends of the measure might entertain. Our situation, also, has been peculiar and difficult. I have found myself surrounded with internal difficulties as well as external dangers. It was my duty, as Executive, to have an eye to every emergency which might possibly arise. My situation might have excused, or even justified, a compromittal on my part, with the hope of securing for my country a respite from existing calamities. I am happy to assure you, however, that I have incurred no committal prejudicial to her interests or my own honor. I am free to take any action which her future welfare may require, and be perfectly vindicated from any imputation of bad faith towards any nation or individual. . . .

I am determined upon immediate annexation to the United States. It is not the result of feeling; nor do I believe that the measure would be as advantageous to Texas, if she had permanent peace, as it is indispensably necessary to the United States. Texas with peace could exist without the U. States; but the U. States cannot, without great hazard to the security of their institutions, exist without Texas. The U. States are one of the rival powers of the earth, and from their importance as well as the peculiarity of their institutions and the extent of their commercial relations, they must expect at no distant day, wars, the object of which will be to prevent their continuance, if possible, as a nation.

Situated as Texas is in point of locality, with peace she has nothing to apprehend for years to come. Other nations would not dread her rivalry, but rather court her friendship for commercial advantage. Her people would have nothing to divert them from their agricultural pursuits. Her advancement in the arts of peace and commerce would be inevitable. With a government requiring trifling expenditure, and a tariff much lower than that of the United States, she would invite the commerce of all nations to her ports (as is already to some extent the case); and while she thus increased the demand for her productions she would drive the manufactures of the United States from her markets, from the fact that American manufacturers could not so well compete with those of Europe. In this way, the immense trade of the Northern Mexican States as well as Texas would fall into the hands of European merchants and pass through our ports and territory. In a few years the loss to the American manufacturer would not be a small amount. But, on the other hand, by annexation, these advantages would be secured to the American merchant to the exclusion of the European; for we should then be but one government. . . .

The exchange of commodities between Texas and Europe, would give rise to a feeling of reciprocal benefit; and there would be nothing in all this to excite national cupidity or jealousy towards her. Thus situated, Texas might remain at peace for a half century: nor is it probable that she would then have war, unless it were with Mexico. Her resources having accumulated for this period, she would have sufficient means and ample capacity to subjugate Mexico whenever she might choose so to do. The efficiency and hardy character of her population would, also, enable wise leaders to render subservient the means of Mexico to her own subjugation—This is an imperfect glance at some of the advantages which Texas might hope for as a separate power.

By immediate annexation we relieve ourselves of the solicitude which we have felt as to our situation: yet that would be no guaranty for immediate peace. Mexico might make annexation a cause of war, and inflict annoyances upon us. It might be some time before the proper aid from the U. States would be available for our defence against incursion. Such an incursion would seriously interrupt our citizens in their peaceful avocations. . . .

There is a sameness or unity in our institutions and national interests in Texas which does not exist in the U. States. All our population is agricultural and we have no sectional institution or diversified interests. It is different in the U. S. Their legislation is embarrassed by these interests. The farming, manufacturing, maritime and mercantile interests all claim the peculiar consideration of the national Congress. Texas, independent, would be free from the agitations arising from this condition of things. The interests of the north and the south, in the U. States render it almost two distinct nations. The question of slavery cannot arise in Texas. One portion of the Republic cannot on this subject be arrayed against another. By annexation we should subject ourselves to the hazard of our tranquility and peace on this subject, which, as a separate power, would not exist. The debt of Texas is a mere "drop in the bucket." Our public domain comprises at least one hundred and fifty millions of acres of arable land, with every delightful variety of climate and every natural advantage which a country of the same extent could possibly enjoy. . . .

I wish to reside in a land where all will be subordinate to

law, and where none dare defy its mandates. I have arrived at that period of life, when I earnestly desire retirement and an assurance that whatever I possess will be secured to me by just laws wisely administered. This privilege I would deem a rich requital for whatever I may have performed useful in life. . . .

A special minister, together with our resident Chargé, has been appointed, with full powers, and despatched to consummate the work of annexation. But that you may be the more perfectly informed of everything interesting connected with the subject, I have directed my Private Secretary and confidential friend, W. D. Miller, Esq., to convey my personal salutations and embraces to you, with authority to communicate everything upon every subject. . . .

Now, my venerated friend, you will perceive that [T]exas is presented to the United States. . . . But if, in the confident hope of the union, she should be rejected, her mortification would be indescribable. She has been sought by the United States, and this is the third time she has consented. Were she now to be spurned, it would forever terminate expectation on her part; and it would then not only be left for the United States to expect that she would seek some other friend, but all Christendom would justify her in a course dictated by necessity and sanctioned by wisdom. However adverse this might be to the wishes or the interests of the United States, in her present situation she could not ponder long. The course adopted by the U. States, if it stop short of annexation, will displease France, irritate England and exasperate Mexico. An effort to postpone it to a more convenient season may be tried in the U. States, to subserve party purposes and make a President; Let them beware! I take it that it is of too great magnitude for any impediment to be interposed to its execution.

That you may live to see your hopes in relation to it crowned with complete success, I sincerely desire. In the event that it speedily takes place, I hope it will afford me an opportu-

nity of visiting you again at the Hermitage. It is the ardent desire
of Mrs. Houston to see the day when you can lay your hand on
our little boy's head and bestow upon him your benediction. Be
assured, General, I should rejoice if circumstances should afford
an opportunity for an event so desirable to us.

Be pleased to make the united salutations of Mrs. Houston
and myself to your family. We unite our prayers for your happiness, and join in the expression of our affectionate regard for
you.

Truly your friend,
SAM HOUSTON

THE KANSAS EMIGRANTS

July 1854

We cross the prairie as of old
  The pilgrims crossed the sea,
To make the West, as they the East,
  The homestead of the free!

We go to rear a wall of men
  On freedom's southern line,
And plant beside the cotton tree
  The rugged northern pine!

We're flowing from our native hills
  As our free rivers flow:
The blessing of our motherland
  Is on us as we go.

We go to plant her common schools
  On distant prairie swells,
And give the Sabbaths of the wild
  The music of her bells.

Upbearing, like the ark of old,
  The Bible in our van,
We go to test the truth of God
  Against the fraud of man.

No pause, nor rest, save where the streams
  That feed the Kansas run,
Save where our Pilgrim gonfalon
  Shall flout the setting sun!

We'll tread the prairie as of old
  Our fathers sailed the sea,
And make the West, as they the East,
  The homestead of the free!

JOHN GREENLEAF WHITTIER

PIONEERS! O PIONEERS!

Come my tan-faced children,
Follow well in order, get your weapons ready,
Have you your pistols? Have you your sharp-edged axes?
Pioneers! O pioneers!

For we cannot tarry here,
We must march my darlings, we must bear the brunt of
    danger,
We the youthful sinewy races, all the rest on us depend,
Pioneers! O pioneers!

O you youths, western youths,
So impatient, full of action, full of manly pride and
    friendship,
Plain I see you western youths, see you tramping with the
    foremost,
Pioneers! O pioneers!

Have the elder races halted?
Do they droop and end their lesson, wearied over there
    beyond the seas,
We take up the task eternal, and the burden and the lesson,
Pioneers! O pioneers!

All the past we leave behind,
We debouch upon a newer mightier world, varied world,
Fresh and strong the world we seize, world of labor and the
    march,
Pioneers! O pioneers!

We detachments steady throwing,
Down the edges, through the passes, up the mountains steep,

Conquering, holding, daring, venturing as we go the
   unknown ways,
            Pioneers! O pioneers!

We primeval forests felling,
We the rivers stemming, vexing we and piercing deep the
   mines within,
We the surface broad surveying, we the virgin soil upheaving,
            Pioneers! O pioneers!

Colorado men are we,
From the peaks gigantic, from the great sierras and the high
   plateaus,
From the mine and from the gully, from the hunting trail we
   come,
            Pioneers! O pioneers!

From Nebraska, from Arkansas,
Central inland race are we, from Missouri, with the
   continental blood intervein'd,
All the hands of comrades clasping, all the Southern, all the
   Northern,
            Pioneers! O pioneers!

O resistless restless race!
O beloved race in all! O my breast aches with tender love for
   all!
O I mourn and yet exult, I am rapt with love for all,
            Pioneers! O pioneers!

Raise the mighty mother mistress,
Waving high the delicate mistress, over all the starry mistress
   (bend your heads all),
Raise the fang'd and warlike mistress, stern, impassive,
   weapon'd mistress,
            Pioneers! O pioneers!

See my children, resolute children,
By those swarms upon our rear we must never yield or falter,
Ages back in ghostly millions frowning there behind us
    urging,
        Pioneers! O pioneers!

On and on the compact ranks,
With accessions ever waiting, with the places of the dead
    quickly fill'd,
Through the battle, through defeat, moving yet and never
    stopping,
        Pioneers! O pioneers!

O to die advancing on!
Are there some of us to droop and die? Has the hour come?
Then upon the march we fittest die, soon and sure the gap is
    fill'd,
        Pioneers! O pioneers!

All the pulses of the world,
Falling in they beat for us, with the western movement beat,
Holding single or together, steady moving to the front, all for
    us,
        Pioneers! O pioneers!

Life's involv'd and varied pageants,
All the forms and shows, all the workmen at their work,
All the seamen and the landsmen, all the masters with their
    slaves,
        Pioneers! O pioneers!

All the hapless silent lovers,
All the prisoners in the prisons, all the righteous and the
    wicked,
All the joyous, all the sorrowing, all the living, all the dying,
        Pioneers! O pioneers!

I too with my soul and body,
We, a curious trio, picking, wandering on our way,
Through these shores amid the shadows, with the apparitions
    pressing,
            Pioneers! O pioneers!

Lo, the darting bowling orb!
Lo, the brother orbs around, all the clustering suns and
    planets,
All the dazzling days, all the mystic nights with dreams,
            Pioneers! O pioneers!

These are of us, they are with us,
All for primal needed work, while the followers there in
    embryo wait behind,
We today's procession heading, we the route for travel
    clearing,
            Pioneers! O pioneers!

O you daughters of the West!
O you young and elder daughters! O you mothers and you
    wives!
Never must you be divided, in our ranks you move united,
            Pioneers! O pioneers!

Minstrels latent on the prairies!
(Shrouded bards of other lands, you may rest, you have done
    your work,)
Soon I hear you coming warbling, soon you rise and tramp
    amid us,
            Pioneers! O pioneers!

Not for delectations sweet,
Not the cushion and the slipper, not the peaceful and the
    studious,

Not the riches safe and palling, not for us the tame
    enjoyment,
        Pioneers! O pioneers!

        Do the feasters gluttonous feast?
Do the corpulent sleepers sleep? Have they lock'd and bolted
    doors?
Still be ours the diet hard, and the blanket on the ground,
        Pioneers! O pioneers!

        Has the night descended?
Was the road of late so toilsome? Did we stop discouraged
    nodding on our way?
Yet a passing hour I yield you in your tracks to pause
    oblivious,
        Pioneers! O pioneers!

        Till with sound of trumpet,
Far, far off the daybreak call—hark! how loud and clear I
    hear it wind,
Swift! to the head of the army!—swift! spring to your places,
        Pioneers! O pioneers!

WALT WHITMAN

NIAGARA

Niagara Falls is a most enjoyable place of resort. The hotels are excellent, and the prices not at all exorbitant. The opportunities for fishing are not surpassed in the country; in fact, they are not even equaled elsewhere. Because, in other localities, certain places in the streams are much better than others; but at Niagara one place is just as good as another, for the reason that the fish do not bite anywhere, and so there is no use in your walking five miles to fish, when you can depend on being just as unsuccessful nearer home. The advantages of this state of things have never heretofore been properly placed before the public.

The weather is cool in summer, and the walks and drives are all pleasant and none of them fatiguing. When you start out to "do" the Falls you first drive down about a mile, and pay a small sum for the privilege of looking down from a precipice into the narrowest part of the Niagara River. A railway "cut" through a hill would be as comely if it had the angry river tumbling and foaming through its bottom. You can descend a staircase here 150 feet down and stand at the edge of the water. After you have done it, you will wonder why you did it; but you will then be too late.

The guide will explain to you, in his bloodcurdling way, how he saw the little steamer, *Maid of the Mist,* descend the fearful rapids—how first one paddle-box was out of sight behind the raging billows and then the other, and at what point it was that her smokestack toppled overboard, and where her planking began to break and part asunder—and how she did finally live through the trip, after accomplishing the incredible feat of traveling seventeen miles in six minutes, or six miles in seventeen minutes, I have really forgotten which. But it was very extraordinary, anyhow. It is worth the price of admission to hear the guide tell the story nine times in succession to different parties and never miss a word or alter a sentence or a gesture.

Then you drive over to Suspension Bridge and divide your misery between the chances of smashing down two hundred feet into the river below and the chances of having the railway train overhead smashing down on to you. Either possibility is discomforting taken by itself, but mixed together, they amount in the aggregate to positive unhappiness.

On the Canada side you drive along the chasm between long ranks of photographers standing guard behind their cameras, ready to make an ostentatious frontispiece of you and your decaying ambulance, and your solemn crate with a hide on it, which you are expected to regard in the light of a horse, and a diminished and unimportant background of sublime Niagara; and a great many people *have* the incredible effrontery or the native depravity to aid and abet this sort of crime.

Any day, in the hands of these photographers, you may see stately pictures of Papa and Mama, Johnny and Bub and Sis, or a couple of country cousins, all smiling vacantly, and all disposed in studied and uncomfortable attitudes in their carriage, and all looming up in their awe-inspiring imbecility before the snubbed and diminished presentment of that majestic presence whose ministering spirits are the rainbows, whose voice is the thunder, whose awful front is veiled in clouds, who was monarch here dead and forgotten ages before this hackful of small reptiles was deemed temporarily necessary to fill a crack in the world's unnoted myriads, and will still be monarch here ages and decades of ages after they shall have gathered themselves to their blood relations, the other worms, and been mingled with the unremembering dust.

There is no actual harm in making Niagara a background whereon to display one's marvelous insignificance in a good strong light, but it requires a sort of superhuman self-complacency to enable one to do it.

When you have examined the stupendous Horseshoe Fall till you are satisfied you cannot improve on it, you return to America by the new Suspension Bridge, and follow up the bank to where they exhibit the Cave of the Winds. Here I followed instructions and divested myself of all my clothing and put on a waterproof jacket and overalls. This costume is picturesque, but not beautiful. A guide, similarly dressed, led the way down a flight of winding stairs, which wound and wound and still kept on winding long after the thing ceased to be a novelty, and then terminated long before it had begun to be a pleasure. We were then well down under the precipice but still considerably above the level of the river.

We now began to creep along flimsy bridges of a single plank, our persons shielded from destruction by a crazy wooden railing, to which I clung with both hands—not because I was afraid, but because I wanted to. Presently the descent became steeper, and the bridge flimsier, and sprays from the American Fall began to rain down on us in fast increasing sheets that soon became blinding, and after that our progress was mostly in the nature of groping. Now a furious wind began to rush out from behind the waterfall, which seemed determined to sweep us from the bridge, and scatter us on the rocks and among the torrents below. I remarked that I wanted to go home; but it was too late. We were almost under the monstrous wall of water thundering down from above, and speech was in vain in the midst of such a pitiless crash of sound.

In another moment the guide disappeared behind the deluge, and, bewildered by the thunder, driven helplessly by the wind, and smitten by the arrowy tempest of rain, I followed. All was darkness. Such a mad storming, roaring, and bellowing of warring wind and water never crazed my ears before. I bent my head, and seemed to receive the Atlantic on my back. The world seemed going to destruction. I could not see anything, the flood poured down so savagely. I raised my head, with open mouth, and the most of the American cataract went down my throat. If I had sprung a leak now I had been lost. And at this moment I discovered that the bridge had ceased, and we must trust for a foothold to the slippery and precipitous rocks. I never was so scared before and survived it. But we got through at last, and emerged into the open day, where we could stand in front of the laced and frothy and seething world of descending water, and look at it. When I saw how much of it there was, and how fearfully in earnest it was, I was sorry I had gone behind it.

MARK TWAIN, c. 1874

YOSEMITE

Sound! sound! sound!
O colossal walls and crown'd
In one eternal thunder!
Sound! sound! sound!
O ye oceans overhead,
While we walk, subdued in wonder,
In the ferns and grasses, under
And beside the swift Merced!

Fret! fret! fret!
Streaming, sounding banners, set
On the giant granite castles
In the clouds and in the snow!
But the foe he comes not yet—
We are loyal, valiant vassals,
And we touch the trailing tassels
Of the banners far below.

Surge! surge! surge!
From the white Sierra's verge,
To the very valley blossom.
Surge! surge! surge!

Yet the songbird builds a home,
And the mossy branches cross them,
And the tasseled treetops toss them
In the clouds of falling foam.

Sweep! sweep! sweep!
O ye heaven-born and deep,
In one dread, unbroken chorus!
We may wonder or may weep—
We may wait on God before us;
We may shout or lift a hand—
We may bow down and deplore us,
But may never understand.

Beat! beat! beat!
We advance, but would retreat
From this restless, broken breast
Of the earth in a convulsion.
We would rest, but dare not rest,
For the angel of expulsion
From this paradise below
Waves us onward and . . . we go.

JOAQUIN MILLER

IN SOUTHERN CALIFORNIA

Where the cocoa and cactus are neighbors,
Where the fig and the fir tree are one;
Where the brave corn is lifting bent sabers
And flashing them far in the sun;

Where maidens blush red in their tresses
Of night, and retreat to advance,
And the dark, sweeping eyelash expresses
Deep passion, half hush'd in a trance;

Where the fig is in leaf, where the blossom
Of orange is fragrant as fair—
Santa Barbara's balm in the bosom,
Her sunny, soft winds in the hair;

Where the grape is most luscious; where laden
Long branches bend double with gold;
Los Angelos leans like a maiden,
Red, blushing, half shy, and half bold.

Where passion was born, and where poets
Are deeper in silence than song,
A love knows a love, and may know its
Reward, yet may never know wrong.

Where passion was born and where blushes
Gave birth to my songs of the South,
And a song is a love-tale, and rushes,
Unchid, through the red of the mouth;

Where an Adam in Eden reposes,
I repose, I am glad, and take wine
In the clambering, redolent roses,
And under my fig and my vine.

JOAQUIN MILLER

THREE SOUTHERN CITIES

CHARLESTON, SOUTH CAROLINA

As one stands upon the steeple of old St. Michael's Church, a sheer hundred feet above any roofs in the neighborhood (where every visitor *should* stand, at his first sallying-forth into the city after arrival, for from here one may gain a complete idea of the entire environment almost at a glance), and looks over the general face of the city, perhaps no impression is more prominent than the thorough gentlemanliness of it. There is nothing "loud" in sight. This gentlemanly aspect is all the more striking in that it exhibits itself under the disadvantage of at least two very unfavorable circumstances. One is that the houses are all turned to a dingy color—even those newly painted—by the unusually strong quality of the sea air which here sweeps freshly in from the near ocean. The other is that the physiognomy of the city is so peculiar as to render it absolutely unlike that of any other city in the world within my knowledge. The houses, with their long three-storied stretches of piazzas, do not front the street, they front the sea breeze; they are all arranged with their ends up the street, precisely like pews in a church.

I have called these disadvantageous circumstances, because it is certainly a severe test of a man's gentlemanly bearing when he preserves it intact in spite of being dressed at once rustily and unlike everybody else.

But Charleston does: its air, as it stands there under the steeple of St. Michael's, is distinctly full of affable decorum; and no visitor with the least perception of the fitness of things can stay in the pleasant old city for a day or two without imbibing this sense of genial old-time dignity, to the extent of wishing that Charleston might always be, as it is, at once sober-suited and queer and delightful.

Going round the balcony of the steeple of St. Michael's to the battery-side, and facing seaward: the river sweeping down on your right is the Cooper; that on the left is the Ashley; as the glance runs down the farther bank of Cooper River seaward, the points of land which last meet the eye represent James and Morris islands, whose batteries were so famous during the war; inclosing the harbor on the left is Sullivan's Island, on which one perceives the town of Moultrieville and Fort Moultrie. In the center view one sees Fort Sumter and, more inland, Castle Pinckney. On the right appears Fort Johnson. . . .

[Charleston] . . . seems to have preserved its individuality in a marvelous degree. One observes with pleasure many signs indicating a return of the commercial importance which the city had gained before the late war. Its old West India trade, which acquired such a lucrative momentum during the Anglo-French wars, is not now so great; but it is being replaced in other ways, notably by increased shipments of lumber and naval stores, due to the new activities in these directions recently inaugurated in South Carolina by the southward movement of lumbermen and distillers who have begun to abandon the worn-out pine forests of North Carolina for the new and comparatively untouched districts of South Carolina, Georgia, and Florida.

Perhaps no city of equal size with Charleston has accumulated so long and brilliant a list of names eminent in diverse departments of activity. . . . As for the fine old merchants, and the fine old planters, who are associated with this city, the enumeration of them would fill a volume. Nothing can be pleasanter—in these days which one would feel strongly inclined to call degenerate did not one have unconquerable faith in the necessary continued bettering of times—than to dwell upon the confident and trustful relations existing between these old planters and merchants, the one producing, the other product-handling, and to trace their roots in the honesties of reputable dealings of many unimpeachable years of trade; and nothing can be more pitiable than that at the time when this amiable outcome of the old Southern civilization became known to the world at large, it became so through being laid bare by the sharp spasm of civil war. That was a time when all our eyes and faces were distorted with passion; none of us either saw, or showed, true. Thrice-pitiable, one says again, that the fairer aspects of a social state which though neither perfect as its violent friends preached nor satanic as its violent enemies denounced yet gave rise to so many beautiful relations of honor and fidelity should have now gone into the past, to remain illuminated only by the unfavorable glare of accidentally associated emotions in which no man can see clearly.

The sojourner in Charleston will find several places of interest to visit. A steamer makes excursions in the winter to the celebrated Middleton Place, where one can see the capacities of this region in the matter of large and brilliant flowers. On Sullivan's Island, the beautiful beach, Fort Moultrie, and the grave of heart-broken Osceola are the objective-points. One must drive or stroll through Rutledge Avenue, which is the Fifth Avenue of Charleston; and Magnolia Cemetery must be seen. The quaint interior of St. Michael's, with its high box-pews and antique suggestions; the old French Protestant Church; the Charleston College museum, an extensive collection, owing its origin to the suggestions of the lamented Agassiz, and intimately associated with the names of Bachman, Audubon, James Hamilton Couper, the Misses Annelly, and Mitchell King; the Charleston Library, a large collection of books which has been maintained by the Charleston Library Society since the year 1748; the antique and often renowned tombs of the old cemeteries of St. Philip's, St. Michael's, the Independent Congregationalist, Unitarian, First and Second Presbyterian, Baptist, German Lutheran, Roman Catholic, Trinity, and Hebrew churches; all offer inducements for the bestowal of one's mornings. Besides these, the historic battlegrounds of Fort Sumter and of James and Morris islands may be made the objective-points of sailing excursions. . . . A pleasant strolling-ground and meeting-place is the Battery, which is laid out in walks and adorned with trees, and commands ample water-prospects; where, if you meet a

Charleston friend, you should get him to tell you the history of the beautiful chime of bells in the belfry of St. Michael's, as you pace up and down the white walks in the gentle air that comes off the near Gulf Stream.

One fares well in the matter of hostelry at Charleston; the Charleston Hotel has long had a delightful reputation among travelers. There are smaller hotels, such as the Victoria, Pavilion, and others. . . .

There are two well-arranged street-railways. That called the Enterprise Railway is specially notable. Its tracks, which the visitor will frequently observe curving off towards the waterfront, connect the principal wharves directly with the railroad depots, so affording extraordinary facilities for the shipment of cotton, rice, naval stores, and the like. Besides these more purely commercial tracks, it has a street line proper, running via Meeting, John, Chapel, Washington, and East Bay streets.

The other street-railway is known as the City Railway and runs two lines of cars—the Rutledge Avenue line and King Street line.

SAVANNAH, GEORGIA

On the first day of February in the year 1733 the city of Savannah, being then but a few hours old, consisted of four tents, which were sufficient for all its inhabitants and were pitched under four pine trees near the edge of the bluff between Bull and Whitaker streets.

It appears that for a year or two previous to this date the attention of certain good and charitable gentlemen of England had been called to the fact that many unfortunate persons were languishing in the debtors' prisons of that country, and that some radical means should be adopted in order to afford new avenues of fortune to poor men and younger sons of families. The interest of these gentlemen finally took the direction of procuring a charter from King George II, granted to them as trustees, authorizing the colonization of a tract lying between the Savannah and Altamaha rivers; and in pursuance thereof James Oglethorpe set sail from Gravesend on the seventeenth of November 1732, with thirty-five families, reaching Charleston, South Carolina, on the thirteenth of February thereafter. Receiving the most cordial assistance from the South Carolinians, the party proceeded to Beaufort, where Oglethorpe left them and went ahead with Colonel William Bull of South Carolina (whose name is perpetuated in Bull Street, one of the most beautiful streets in America, and the present fashionable promenade of Savannah) to select a site for the city, which it had been previously determined to locate on the Savannah River. . . .

Truly an Arcadian city! It would really seem that these broad and noble ideas which thus came like good fairies to the birth of Savannah and contributed their gifts to it have never withdrawn themselves from watching over the further growth of the city. Perhaps no town of equal age has more clearly preserved the general plans and spirit of its founders. Here the visitor of today still sees the wide symmetrical streets, the generous and frequent squares, the lavish adornment of grasses, flowers, and magnificent trees, which appear to render into material form the liberal and manly tone of Oglethorpe's inaugural management; and every one acquainted with the modes of Savannah life among its best citizens will recognize the spirit of quiet refinement, the reserve, the absence of ostentation which Francis Moore has commemorated in the opening words of the extract above given. The residences, many of which are very beautiful, appear to withdraw themselves from observation, and to hide behind their wide piazzas and balconies which are inclosed with Venetian blinds; and one may stroll along the pleasant promenade of Bull Street, or through the alleys of Forsyth Park, for a whole afternoon without encountering a lady dressed "loudly." . . .

There are many points of interest to visit. Sailboats are always to be obtained for excursions down the river; and there is a small railway, connecting at Bolton with the streetcars, upon which one can with facility reach Thunderbolt, a noted spot on the river five miles from town where in the warm afternoons the owners of fine teams cluster on the pleasant riverbank under the trees ere turning about for the drive back to the city. A shell-road reaches to Thunderbolt which forms The Drive of Savannah and is a gay enough thoroughfare on pleasant afternoons. A road turns off to the left from this shell-road and leads to the famous old burying-place called Bonaventure, a spot about a mile from Thunderbolt which no one sojourning at Savannah should fail to visit. . . .

Savannah is one of the most prosperous cities in the Union and is a port of growing commercial importance. The great exports are cotton, lumber, and rice; and the activities incident to the handling of the large quantities of these staples which are here annually received make it a busy city in the fall and winter. It is the terminus of several railways. . . . There are also several lines of steamships to New York, one to Philadelphia, and one to Baltimore; a coast-line to Charleston; . . . [and] one to Augusta, on the Savannah River. . . . An important feeder of the city is the Savannah and Ogeechee Canal, extending between the Savannah and Ogeechee rivers.

The city has a notable number of benevolent institutions; an admirable public school system; a fine antiquarian association known as the Georgia Historical Society, which has just erected a very handsome library building and has recently come into a large bequest from the late Miss Mary Telfair; and a number of well-built churches, particularly the Independent Presbyterian, with the lofty spire, fronting on Bull Street. The city is furnished with waterworks, which supply water from the Savannah River.

And lastly, its police headquarters is precisely the police headquarters which one would expect in an Arcadian city: being a plain building in a cool and shady brick court, overhung by trees, covered with climbing vines, and, to the view of the passerby at least, as clean as a Dutch parlor.

JACKSONVILLE, FLORIDA

Jacksonville and St. Augustine are two cities not fifty miles apart; but the difference between them is just the distance from the nineteenth century to the sixteenth. . . . Nothing can seem more appropriate than their names; for the former strikes you with all the vim of Andrew Jackson, after whom it is called, while about the latter you cannot fail to find a flavor of saintly contemplation which seems to breathe from out the ancient name of the good old father whom Menendez selected for its patron saint.

Jacksonville not only belongs to the nineteenth century but practically to the last ten years. . . . For previous to the war between the states it was a comparatively insignificant town, and even after the war, in the year 1866, I am informed that a careful census made under the auspices of the Freedman's Bureau revealed but about seventeen hundred inhabitants in it, a majority of whom are said to have been Negroes drawing their main subsistence from the charities of the nation. The resident population is now between twelve and fourteen thousand, and this number is largely increased during the winter. It bears all the signs of a city prospering upon the legitimate bases of an admirable commercial location and of an enterprising body of citizens; and in midwinter offers to the Northern visitor a pleasant surprise, which coming after the railway journey through the pines is almost like a romantic adventure after a long stretch of quiet life. The train comes to a stop on the wharf: as one steps from the car, one hears a pleasant plash among the lily pads underneath the platform, and, lifting the eyes at this suggestion of waters, perceives the great placid expanses of the St. Johns stretching far away to the south and east. A few yards from the railway station, across Bay Street, the long façade of the Grand National Hotel elevates itself; wherefrom, if the traveler's *entrée* be at night, he is like to hear sounds of music coming, through brilliantly lighted windows opening upon a wide balcony where many people are promenading in the pleasant evening air. Farther back in the town a few hundred yards, situated among fine oaks which border a newly planted open square, is the St. James Hotel; where the chances are strong that as one peeps through the drawing-room windows on the way to one's room, one will find so many New York faces and Boston faces and Chicago faces that one does not feel so very far from home after all.

The Grand National and the St. James are open only during the winter; and when we came along back this way in the late spring we found rough planks barring their hospitalities up—a clear case, in fact, of roses shutting and being buds again. . . . The Metropolitan Hotel, a quarter of a mile downtown from the depot, between Bay Street and Forsyth, blooms all the year round. . . .

Minor hostelries of various sorts are said to amount to one hundred in number. The National and St. James charge four dollars a day, the Metropolitan three; the smaller houses from one and a half to three a day, and from ten to twenty dollars a week. As one emerges from one's hotel in the morning, upon those springy plank sidewalks which constitute a sort of strolls-made-easy over a large part of the city, one is immediately struck with the splendid young water-oaks which border the streets, sometimes completely arching them over. Their foliage is dense, and, what with the brilliance of the sun, the lights and shadows are right Rembrandt. These trees contrast greatly with the pines through which one has been traveling ever since one left Wilmington, and in the midst of great forests of which Jacksonville itself is situated. . . .

A subtle sense of multitude begins to reveal itself to him who stands among the great pine forests. We are accustomed to speak of the multitude of the stars: the astronomers say there are only about six thousand of them visible on a clear night to the naked eye; but six thousand pines! Six thousand is only the insignificant content of a few acres: here are thousands of square miles of them. . . .

At this hour of the morning in Jacksonville everybody is eating his antebreakfast oranges, with as much vigor as if he saw himself growing suddenly wrinkled and flaccid, like the gods and goddesses in Wagner's *Rheingold* when they had in their agitation forgotten to eat their daily allowance of the golden fruit which grew in Freya's garden and which was the necessary condition of their immortal youth. . . .

But the sight of your dripping fingers reminds one that while there are few pleasanter things than the eating of an orange, yet it is also in the order of nature that difficulty and delight—which are essentially birds of a feather—should fly together, and there are therefore few harder things than the eating of an orange dry-fingered. The stickiness of orange juice seems somehow at once one of the most unavoidable and most disagreeable of the earthly bads that hang by the goods. . . .

By this time, no matter in what direction we may have started, we will have arrived in Bay Street, which runs parallel with and next to the river. It is the main business street of the city, and is a lively enough thoroughfare of a winter's morning. The curious visitors are trooping everywhere along the sidewalks—to the post office, to the fruit stores, to the palmetto-braiders', to the curiosity shops, to the wharf for a sailboat, to the fizzing steamboats for a trip up the St. Johns or the Ocklawaha. The merchants and shopkeepers are all busy. Along with the noises of traffic comes the hum of the lumber mills; fitly enough, for the latter are said to conduce no little to the prosperity of the former, in bringing about cheap freights. The three-masted schooners that you see lying at the wharves there, waiting for cargoes of lumber, will transport heavy goods at almost any price when they come here, rather than sail in ballast.

The visitor strolling down this street soon discovers that not an inconsiderable item in the commerce of Jacksonville is the trade in "Florida curiosities," to which he will find several establishments devoted. These curiosities are sea-beans, alligators' teeth, plumes of herons' and curlews' feathers, cranes' wings, angel-fish, mangrove and orange walking-canes, coral branches, coquina-figures, and many others. . . .

Jacksonville is as it were a city built to order, and many

provisions have been made for employing the leisure of its winter visitors. A very good circulating library is to be found on the northern side of Bay Street, a short distance below the National Hotel, which is open to strangers for borrowing; and a lively news-vender in the same room supplies all the prominent current papers and magazines every morning. A pleasant sort of exchange for visitors is also to be found in the reading-room of Ambler's Bank, farther down Bay Street, on the opposite side. Beyond this, a few doors, is the post office. At the sign "Boats to let," on the wharf, not far below the Grand National, one can find pleasant sailboats for hire at prices ranging from seventy-five cents an hour upward.

Several good livery stables offer first-class turnouts, in the way of saddle-horses, buggies, and carriages; and there are two shell-roads which afford pleasant drives. A very good objective-point for a ride is Moncrief's Spring. This is a mineral spring, not yet analyzed, but said to be of often-tested efficacy in the cure of intermittent fevers and of agues. It lies about four miles from town, near a creek also called Moncrief. The water is unusually transparent, and is first received in a circular basin twenty feet in diameter. Below this, well-arranged bathhouses, separate for ladies and gentlemen, each sixty feet long by fifteen wide, are being built. A restaurant, bowling alley, dancing-pavilion, and racecourse of a mile in length are also in process of construction. On the way to this spring one passes through the pleasant suburb known as Springfield.

From the high ground here a good view may be obtained of Jacksonville and the river. The hill slopes down to Hogan's Creek, a boundary line of the city. Besides Springfield, the advancing growth of Jacksonville has developed several other named suburbs, such as East Jacksonville, Oakland, Wyoming, La Villa, Brooklyn, Riverside, South Shore, and Alexandria.

SIDNEY LANIER,
from *Florida*, 1876

THE FOUNDERS OF OHIO

The footsteps of a hundred years
   Have echoed, since o'er Braddock's Road
Bold Putnam and the pioneers
   Led history the way they strode.

On wild Monongahela stream
   They launched the Mayflower of the West,
A perfect state their civic dream,
   A New World their pilgrim quest.

When April robed the Buckeye trees
   Muskingum's bosky shore they trod;
They pitched their tents, and to the breeze
   Flung freedom's star-flag, thanking God.

As glides the Oyo's solemn flood,
   So fleeted their eventful years;
Resurgent in their children's blood,
   They still live on—the pioneers.

Their fame shrinks not to names and dates
   On votive stone, the prey of time—
Behold where monumental states
   Immortalize their lives sublime!

WILLIAM HENRY VENABLE

SONG OF THE CHATTAHOOCHEE

Out of the hills of Habersham,
  Down the valleys of Hall,
I hurry amain to reach the plain,
Run the rapid and leap the fall,
Split at the rock and together again,
Accept my bed, or narrow or wide,
And flee from folly on every side
With a lover's pain to attain the plain
  Far from the hills of Habersham,
  Far from the valleys of Hall.

All down the hills of Habersham,
  All through the valleys of Hall,
The rushes cried, *Abide, abide,*
The willful waterweeds held me thrall,
The laving laurel turned my tide,
The ferns and the fondling grass said, *Stay,*
The dewberry dipped for to work delay,
And the little reeds sighed, *Abide, abide,*
  Here in the hills of Habersham,
  Here in the valleys of Hall.

High o'er the hills of Habersham,
  Veiling the valleys of Hall,
The hickory told me manifold
Fair tales of shade, the poplar tall
Wrought me her shadowy self to hold,
The chestnut, the oak, the walnut, the pine,
Overleaning, with flickering meaning and sign,
Said, *Pass not, so cold, these manifold*
  Deep shades of the hills of Habersham,
  These glades in the valleys of Hall.

And oft in the hills of Habersham,
   And oft in the valleys of Hall,
The white quartz shone, and the smooth brook-stone
Did bar me of passage with friendly brawl,
And many a luminous jewel lone—
Crystals clear or a-cloud with mist,
Ruby, garnet and amethyst—
Made lures with the lights of streaming stone
   In the clefts of the hills of Habersham,
   In the beds of the valleys of Hall.

But oh, not the hills of Habersham,
   And oh, not the valleys of Hall
Avail: I am fain for to water the plain.
Downward the voices of Duty call—
Downward, to toil and be mixed with the main,
The dry fields burn, and the mills are to turn,
And a myriad flowers mortally yearn,
And the lordly main from beyond the plain
   Calls o'er the hills of Habersham,
   Calls through the valleys of Hall.

SIDNEY LANIER

THE AMERICAN FORESTS

The forests of America, however slighted by man, must have been a great delight to God; for they were the best He ever planted. The whole continent was a garden, and from the beginning it seemed to be favored above all the other wild parks and gardens of the globe. To prepare the ground, it was rolled and sifted in seas with infinite loving deliberation and forethought, lifted into the light, submerged and warmed over and over again, pressed and crumpled into folds and ridges, mountains, and hills, subsoiled with heaving volcanic fires, ploughed and ground and sculptured into scenery and soil with glaciers and rivers—every feature growing and changing from beauty to beauty, higher and higher. And in the fullness of time it was planted in groves, and belts, and broad, exuberant, mantling forests, with the largest, most varied, most fruitful, and most beautiful trees in the world. Bright seas made its border, with wave embroidery and icebergs; gray deserts were outspread in the middle of it, mossy tundras on the north, savannas on the south, and blooming prairies and plains; while lakes and rivers shone through all the vast forests and openings, and happy birds and beasts gave delightful animation. Everywhere, everywhere over all the blessed continent, there were beauty and melody and kindly, wholesome, foodful abundance.

These forests were composed of about five hundred species of trees, all of them in some way useful to man, ranging in size from twenty-five feet in height and less than one foot in diameter at the ground to four hundred feet in height and more than twenty feet in diameter—lordly monarchs proclaiming the gospel of beauty like apostles. . . . Wide-branching oak and elm in endless variety, walnut and maple, chestnut and beech, ilex and locust, touching limb to limb, spread a leafy translucent canopy along the coast of the Atlantic over the wrinkled folds and ridges of the Alleghenies—a green billowy sea in summer, golden and purple in autumn, pearly gray like a steadfast frozen mist of interlacing branches and sprays in leafless, restful winter.

To the southward stretched dark, level-topped cypresses in knobby, tangled swamps, grassy savannas in the midst of them like lakes of light, groves of gay, sparkling spice trees, magnolias and palms, glossy-leaved and blooming and shining continually. To the northward, over Maine and Ottawa, rose hosts of spiry, rosiny evergreens—white pine and spruce, hemlock and cedar, shoulder to shoulder, laden with purple cones, their myriad needles sparkling and shimmering, covering hills and swamps, rocky headlands and domes, ever bravely aspiring and seeking the sky; the ground in their shade now snow-clad and frozen, now mossy and flowery; beaver meadows here and there, full of lilies and grass; lakes gleaming like eyes, and a silvery embroidery of rivers and creeks watering and brightening all the vast glad wilderness.

Thence westward were oak and elm, hickory and tupelo, gum and liriodendron, sassafras and ash, linden and laurel, spreading on ever wider in glorious exuberance over the great fertile basin of the Mississippi, over damp level bottoms, low dimpling hollows, and round dotting hills, embosoming sunny prairies and cheery park openings, half sunshine, half shade; while a dark wilderness of pines covered the region around the Great Lakes. Thence still westward swept the forests to right and left around grassy plains and deserts a thousand miles wide: irrepressible hosts of spruce and pine, aspen and willow, nut-pine and juniper, cactus and yucca, caring nothing for drought, extending undaunted from mountain to mountain, over mesa and desert, to join the darkening multitudes of pines that covered the high Rocky ranges and the glorious forests along the coast of the moist and balmy Pacific, where new species of pine, giant cedars and spruces, silver firs and sequoias, kings of their race, growing close together like grass in a meadow, poised their brave domes and spires in the sky, three hundred feet above the ferns and the lilies that enameled the ground; towering serene through the long centuries, preaching God's forestry fresh from heaven.

Here the forests reached their highest development. Hence they went wavering northward over icy Alaska, brave spruce and fir, poplar and birch, by the coasts and the rivers, to within sight of the Arctic Ocean. American forests! the glory of the world! Surveyed thus from the east to the west, from the north. to the south, they are rich beyond thought, immortal, immeasurable, enough and to spare for every feeding, sheltering beast and bird, insect and son of Adam; and nobody need have cared had there been no pines in Norway, no cedars and deodars on Lebanon and the Himalayas, no vine-clad selvas in the basin of the Amazon. With such variety, harmony, and triumphant exuberance, even nature, it would seem, might have rested content with the forests of North America, and planted no more.

So they appeared a few centuries ago when they were rejoicing in wildness. The Indians with stone axes could do them no more harm than could gnawing beavers and browsing moose. Even the fires of the Indians and the fierce shattering lightning seemed to work together only for good in clearing spots here and there for smooth garden prairies, and openings for sunflowers seeking the light. But when the steel axe of the white man rang out on the startled air their doom was sealed. Every tree heard the bodeful sound, and pillars of smoke gave the sign in the sky. . . .

It seems . . . that almost every civilized nation can give us a lesson on the management and care of forests. So far our government has done nothing effective with its forests, though the best in the world, but is like a rich and foolish spendthrift who has inherited a magnificent estate in perfect order, and then has left his fields and meadows, forests and parks, to be sold and plundered and wasted at will, depending on their inexhaustible abundance. Now it is plain that the forests are not inexhaustible, and that quick measures must be taken if ruin is to be avoided. Year by year the remnant is growing smaller before the axe and fire, while the laws in existence provide neither for the protection of the timber from destruction nor for its use where it is most needed. . . .

That a change from robbery and ruin to a permanent rational policy is urgently needed nobody with the slightest knowledge of American forests will deny. In the East and along the northern Pacific coast, where the rainfall is abundant, comparatively few care keenly what becomes of the trees so long as fuel and lumber are not noticeably dear. But in the Rocky Mountains and California and Arizona, where the forests are inflammable, and where the fertility of the lowlands depends upon irrigation, public opinion is growing stronger every year in favor of permanent protection by the federal government of all the forests that cover the sources of the streams. . . .

The redwood is the glory of the Coast Range. It extends along the western slope, in a nearly continuous belt about ten miles wide, from beyond the Oregon boundary to the south of Santa Cruz, a distance of nearly four hundred miles, and in massive, sustained grandeur and closeness of growth surpasses all the other timber woods of the world. Trees from 10 to 15 feet in diameter and 300 feet high are not uncommon, and a few attain a height of 350 feet or even 400, with a diameter at the base of 15 to 20 feet or more, while the ground beneath them is a garden of fresh, exuberant ferns, lilies, gaultheria, and rhododendron. . . .

Notwithstanding all the waste and use which have been going on unchecked like a storm for more than two centuries, it is not yet too late—though it is high time—for the government to begin a rational administration of its forests. About seventy million acres it still owns—enough for all the country, if wisely used. These residual forests are generally on mountain slopes, just where they are doing the most good, and where their removal would be followed by the greatest number of evils; the lands they cover are too rocky and high for agriculture, and can never be made as valuable for any other crop as for the present crop of trees. . . .

In their natural condition, or under wise management, keeping out destructive sheep, preventing fires, selecting the trees that should be cut for lumber, and preserving the young ones and the shrubs and sod of herbaceous vegetation, these forests would be a never failing fountain of wealth and beauty. The cool shades of the forest give rise to moist beds and currents of air, and the sod of grasses and the various flowering plants and shrubs thus fostered, together with the network and sponge of tree roots, absorb and hold back the rain and the waters from melting snow, compelling them to ooze and percolate and flow gently through the soil in streams that never dry. . . .

The wonderful advance made in the last few years in creating four national parks in the West, and thirty forest reservations, embracing nearly forty million acres; and in the planting of the borders of streets and highways and spacious parks in all the great cities, to satisfy the natural taste and hunger for landscape beauty and righteousness that God has put, in some measure, into every human being and animal, shows the trend of awakening public opinion. The making of the far-famed New York Central Park was opposed by even good men, with misguided pluck, perseverance, and ingenuity; but straight right won its way, and now that park is appreciated. So we confidently believe it will be with our great national parks and forest reservations. . . .

It took more than three thousand years to make some of the trees in these western woods—trees that are still standing in perfect strength and beauty, waving and singing in the mighty forests of the Sierra. Through all the wonderful, eventful centuries since Christ's time—and long before that—God has cared for these trees, saved them from drought, disease, avalanches, and a thousand straining, leveling tempests and floods; but he cannot save them from fools—only Uncle Sam can do that.

JOHN MUIR,
from *Our National Parks*, 1901

HYMN OF THE WEST

World's Fair, St. Louis, Missouri, 1904

O thou, whose glorious orbs on high
  Engird the earth with splendor round,
From out Thy secret place draw nigh
   The courts and temples of this ground;
     Eternal Light,
     Fill with Thy might
These domes that in Thy purpose grew,
And lift a nation's heart anew!

Illumine Thou each pathway here,
  To show the marvels God hath wrought!
Since first Thy people's chief and seer
   Looked up with that prophetic thought,
     Bade Time unroll
     The fateful scroll,
And empire unto Freedom gave
From cloudland height to tropic wave.

Poured through the gateways of the North
  Thy mighty rivers join their tide,
And, on the wings of morn sent forth,
   Their mists the far-off peaks divide.
     By Thee unsealed,
     The mountains yield
Ores that the wealth of Ophir shame,
And gems enwrought of seven-hued flame.

Lo, through what years the soil hath lain,
  At Thine own time to give increase—
The greater and the lesser grain,

164

The ripening boll, the myriad fleece!
   Thy creatures graze
   Appointed ways;
League after league across the land
The ceaseless herds obey Thy hand.

Thou, whose high archways shine most clear
  Above the plenteous western plain,
Thine ancient tribes from round the sphere
  To breathe its quickening air are fain:
    And smiles the sun
    To see made one
Their brood throughout earth's greenest space,
Land of the new and lordlier race!

               EDMUND CLARENCE STEDMAN

NEW YORK

She sits beside the ocean,
With a river on either hand,
And all the wealth of waters
By giant girdles spanned.

Like messengers of gladness
The swift sails come and go,
Full-freighted with a promise
The hungry world should know,

Since to earth's farthest limits
They bear the precious spoil

Wrung from the gold-paved caverns,
Brought from the teeming soil.

Voices of many nations
Make music in the streets,
Their blooded pulses quicken
The heart that steadfast beats.

Brave blood she brought from Britain,
From Holland careful thrift,
And ancient empires taught her
Their wisdom and uplift.

She yields to helpful labor
Its meed and honor fit,
And in her princely mansions
The peasant's son may sit.

God grant our noble city
Forever thus to stand,
A sentinel of freedom,
Guarding a blessed land.

JULIA WARD HOWE

CHICAGO

Hog Butcher for the World,
Tool Maker, Stacker of Wheat,
Player with Railroads and the Nation's
    Freight Handler;
Stormy, husky, brawling,
City of the Big Shoulders:

They tell me you are wicked and I believe them, for
    I have seen your painted women under the gas
    lamps luring the farm boys.
And they tell me you are crooked and I answer:
    Yes, it is true I have seen the gunman kill and
    go free to kill again.
And they tell me you are brutal and my reply is:
    On the faces of women and children I have
    seen the marks of wanton hunger.
And having answered so I turn once more to those
    who sneer at this my city, and I give them
    back the sneer and say to them:
Come and show me another city with lifted head
    singing so proud to be alive and coarse and
    strong and cunning.
Flinging magnetic curses amid the toil of piling job
    on job, here is a tall bold slugger set vivid
    against the little soft cities;
Fierce as a dog with tongue lapping for action,
    cunning as a savage pitted against the wilder-
    ness,
        Bareheaded,
        Shoveling,
        Wrecking,
        Planning,
        Building, breaking, rebuilding,

Under the smoke, dust all over his mouth, laughing
 with white teeth,
Under the terrible burden of destiny laughing as a
 young man laughs,
Laughing even as an ignorant fighter laughs who
 has never lost a battle,
Bragging and laughing that under his wrist is
 the pulse, and under his ribs the heart of the
 people,
 Laughing!
Laughing the stormy, husky, brawling laughter of
 Youth, half-naked, sweating, proud to be
 Hog Butcher, Tool Maker, Stacker of Wheat,
 Player with Railroads and Freight Handler to
 the Nation.

CARL SANDBURG

PART FOUR

---- ★ ----

The Social Fabric

AS PEOPLE from England, Europe, Asia, and Africa and Native Americans struggled to establish their places in the territory of America, their experiences and decisions were reflected in poetry, essays, and documents. During the colonial period, a slave, Phillis Wheatley, wrote poetry that was much admired by Thomas Jefferson and other intellectuals; her "On Being Brought from Africa to America" describes how she embraced American Christianity. Jefferson, writing in *Notes on Virginia* in 1784, recognized both the immorality and systemic poison of slavery. The continued toleration of this ignoble institution gave birth to antislavery societies, whose righteous outrage is reflected in abolitionist William Lloyd Garrison's poem "Liberty for All." The tolling of bells marking the adoption in 1865 of the Constitution's Thirteenth Amendment, abolishing slavery, inspired John Greenleaf Whittier's poem "Laus Deo!"

Coexistence with the nations of people who had long occupied the land now settled by new Americans remained a major concern throughout the nineteenth century. The problem was addressed by President Andrew Jackson in 1835 with the creation of a reservation in the West, and in 1881 by President Chester A. Arthur, whose policy encouraged Native-American integration into U.S. society.

Women's rights, often associated with abolitionist sentiments and societies, remained an important social issue in the nineteenth century. One of its finest expressions was the Resolutions of the Seneca Falls Women's Rights Convention in 1848;

the Nineteenth Amendment to the Constitution finally established female suffrage in 1920.

Other social issues continued to inspire significant speeches
and documents into the twentieth century. Theodore Roosevelt's famous "Man with the Muck-Rake" speech castigated the
yellow-journalism school of social justice while criticizing the
abuses of large corporations. The rights of the working person
were furthered by such organizations as the American Federation of Labor, whose constitution was ratified in 1932. Religious
tolerance was championed eloquently by Thomas Jefferson and
passionately by U.S. Senator James A. Reed. Responding to the
economic upheaval of the Great Depression, President Franklin
Roosevelt created landmark social legislation with the National
Recovery Act and the Social Security Act. And the issue of civil
rights, still festering so many years after the Civil War, inspired
history-making efforts by the Truman and Johnson administrations.

On Being Brought from Africa
to America

'Twas mercy brought me from my pagan land,
Taught my benighted soul to understand
That there's a God, that there's a Savior too:
Once I redemption neither sought nor knew.
Some view our sable race with scornful eye,
"Their color is a diabolic dye."
Remember Christians; Negroes, black as Cain,
May be refin'd, and join th' angelic train.

PHILLIS WHEATLEY

On Religion

The legitimate powers of government extend to such acts only
as are injurious to others. But it does me no injury for my
neighbor to say there are twenty gods, or no God. It neither
picks my pocket nor breaks my leg. If it be said, his testimony
in a court of justice cannot be relied on, reject it then, and be the
stigma on him. Constraint may make him worse by making him
a hypocrite, but it will never make him a truer man. It may fix
him obstinately in his errors, but will not cure them. Reason and
free inquiry are the only effectual agents against error. Give a
loose to them, they will support the true religion by bringing
every false one to their tribunal, to the test of their investigation.
They are the natural enemies of error and of error only. Had not
the Roman government permitted free inquiry, Christianity
could never have been introduced. Had not free inquiry been

indulged at the era of the Reformation, the corruptions of Christianity could not have been purged away. If it be restrained now, the present corruptions will be protected, and new ones encouraged.

Was the government to prescribe to us our medicine and diet, our bodies would be in such keeping as our souls are now. Thus in France the emetic was once forbidden as a medicine, and the potato as an article of food. Government is just as infallible, too, when it fixed systems in physics. Galileo was sent to the Inquisition for affirming that the earth was a sphere; the government had declared it to be as flat as a trencher, and Galileo was obliged to abjure his error. This error, however, at length prevailed, the earth became a globe, and Descartes declared it was whirled round its axis by a vortex. The government in which he lived was wise enough to see that this was no question of civil jurisdiction, or we should all have been involved by authority in vortices. In fact, the vortices have been exploded, and the Newtonian principle of gravitation is now more firmly established, on the basis of reason, than it would be were the government to step in, and to make it an article of necessary faith.

Reason and experiment have been indulged, and error has fled before them. It is error alone which needs the support of government. Truth can stand by itself. Subject opinion to coercion: whom will you make your inquisitors? Fallible men; men governed by bad passions, by private as well as public reasons. And why subject it to coercion? To produce uniformity. But is uniformity of opinion desirable? No more than of face and stature. Introduce the bed of Procrustes then, and as there is danger that the large men may beat the small, make us all of a size, by lopping the former and stretching the latter. Difference of opinion is advantageous in religion. The several sects perform the office of a *censor morum* over such other. Is uniformity attainable? Millions of innocent men, women, and children, since the introduction of Christianity, have been burnt, tortured, fined, imprisoned; yet we have not advanced one inch toward uniformity. What has been the effect of coercion? To make one-half the world fools, and the other half hypocrites, to support roguery and error all over the earth. Let us reflect that it is inhabited by a thousand millions of people. That these profess probably a thousand different systems of religion. That ours is but one of that thousand. That if there be but one right, and ours that one, we should wish to see the 999 wandering sects gathered into the fold of truth. But against such a majority we cannot effect this by force. Reason and persuasion are the only practicable instruments. To make way for these, free inquiry must be indulged; and how can we wish others to indulge it while we refuse it ourselves. But every state, says an inquisitor, has established some religion. No two, say I, have established the same. Is this a proof of the infallibility of establishments? Our sister states of Pennsylvania and New York, however, have long subsisted without any establishment at all. The experiment was new and doubtful when they made it. It has answered beyond conception. They flourish infinitely. Religion is well supported; of various kinds, indeed, but all good enough; all sufficient to preserve peace and order; or if a sect arises, whose tenets should subvert morals, good sense has fair play, and reasons and laughs it out of doors, without suffering the state to be troubled with it. They do not hang more malefactors than we do. They are not more disturbed with religious dissensions. On the contrary, their harmony is unparalleled, and can be ascribed to nothing but their unbounded tolerance, because there is no other circumstance in which they differ from every nation on earth. They have made the happy discovery that the way to silence religious disputes is to take no notice of them.

THOMAS JEFFERSON,
from *Notes on Virginia,* 1784

On Slavery

There must doubtless be an unhappy influence on the manners of our people produced by the existence of slavery among us. The whole commerce between master and slave is a perpetual exercise of the most boisterous passions, the most unremitting despotism on the one part, and degrading submissions on the other. Our children see this, and learn to imitate it; for man is an imitative animal. This quality is the germ of all education in him. From his cradle to his grave he is learning to do what he sees others do. If a parent could find no motive either in his philanthropy or his self-love for restraining the intemperance of passion toward his slave, it should always be a sufficient one that his child is present. But generally it is not sufficient. The parent storms, the child looks on, catches the lineaments of wrath, puts on the same airs in the circle of smaller slaves, gives a loose to the worst of passions, and thus nursed, educated, and daily exercised in tyranny, cannot but be stamped by it with odious peculiarities. The man must be a prodigy who can retain his manners and morals undepraved by such circumstances.

And with what execration should the statesman be loaded, who, permitting one-half the citizens thus to trample on the rights of the other, transforms those into despots, and these into enemies, destroys the morals of the one part, and the *amor patriae* of the other. For if a slave can have a country in this world, it must be any other in preference to that in which he is born to live and labor for another; in which he must lock up the faculties of his nature, contribute as far as depends on his individual endeavors to the evanishment of the human race, or entail his own miserable condition on the endless generations proceeding from him. With the morals of the people, their industry also is destroyed. For in a warm climate, no man will labor for himself who can make another labor for him. . . .

And can the liberties of a nation be thought secure when we have removed their only firm basis, a conviction in the minds of the people that these liberties are of the gift of God? That they are not to be violated but with His wrath? Indeed, I tremble for my country when I reflect that God is just; that His justice cannot sleep forever; that considering numbers, nature, and natural means only, a revolution of the wheel of fortune, an exchange of situation is among possible events; that it may become probable by supernatural interference! The Almighty has no attribute which can take side with us in such a contest.

But it is impossible to be temperate and to pursue this subject through the various considerations of policy, of morals, of history natural and civil. We must be contented to hope they will force their way into every one's mind. I think a change already perceptible, since the origin of the present revolution. The spirit of the master is abating, that of the slave rising from the dust, his condition mollifying, the way I hope preparing, under the auspices of heaven, for a total emancipation, and that this is disposed, in the order of events, to be with the consent of the masters, rather than by their extirpation.

THOMAS JEFFERSON,
from *Notes on Virginia*, 1784

THE INDIAN BURYING-GROUND

In spite of all the learned have said,
  I still my old opinion keep;
The posture, that we give the dead,
  Points out the soul's eternal sleep.

Not so the ancients of these lands—
  The Indian, when from life released,
Again is seated with his friends,
  And shares again the joyous feast.

His imaged birds, and painted bowl,
　　And venison, for a journey dressed,
Bespeak the nature of the soul,
　　Activity, that knows no rest.

His bow, for action ready bent,
　　And arrows, with a head of stone,
Can only mean that life is spent,
　　And not the old ideas gone.

Here still a lofty rock remains,
　　On which the curious eye may trace
(Now wasted, half, by wearing rains)
　　The fancies of a ruder race.

Here still an aged elm aspires,
　　Beneath whose far-projecting shade
(And which the shepherd still admires)
　　The children of the forest played!

There oft a restless Indian queen
　　(Pale Shebah, with her braided hair)
And many a barbarous form is seen
　　To chide the man that lingers there.

By midnight moons, o'er moistening dews;
　　In habit for the chase arrayed,
The hunter still the deer pursues,
　　The hunter and the deer, a shade!

And long shall timorous fancy see
　　The painted chief, and pointed spear,
And Reason's self shall bow the knee
　　To shadows and delusions here.

PHILIP FRENEAU

THE REMOVAL OF NATIVE-AMERICAN TRIBES TO A RESERVATION WEST OF THE MISSISSIPPI RIVER

President Andrew Jackson's Seventh Annual Message to Congress, December 7, 1835

All preceding experiments for the improvement of the Indians have failed. It seems now to be an established fact that they cannot live in contact with a civilized community and prosper. Ages of fruitless endeavors have at length brought us to a knowledge of this principle of intercommunication with them. The past we cannot recall, but the future we can provide for. Independently of the treaty stipulations into which we have entered with the various tribes for the usufructuary rights they have ceded to us, no one can doubt the moral duty of the government of the United States to protect and if possible to preserve and perpetuate the scattered remnants of this race which are left within our borders. In the discharge of this duty an extensive region in the West has been assigned for their permanent residence. It has been divided into districts and allotted among them. Many have already removed and others are preparing to go, and with the exception of two small bands living in Ohio and Indiana, not exceeding fifteen hundred persons, and of the Cherokees, all the tribes on the east side of the Mississippi, and extending from Lake Michigan to Florida, have entered into engagements which will lead to their transplantation.

The plan for their removal and reestablishment is founded upon the knowledge we have gained of their character and habits and has been dictated by a spirit of enlarged liberality. A territory exceeding in extent that relinquished has been granted to each tribe. Of its climate, fertility, and capacity to support an

Indian population the representations are highly favorable. To these districts the Indians are removed at the expense of the United States, and with certain supplies of clothing, arms, ammunition, and other indispensable articles; they are also furnished gratuitously with provisions for the period of a year after their arrival at their new homes. In that time, from the nature of the country and of the products raised by them, they can subsist themselves by agricultural labor, if they choose to resort to that mode of life; if they do not they are upon the skirts of the great prairies, where countless herds of buffalo roam, and a short time suffices to adapt their own habits to the changes which a change of the animals destined for their food may require.

Ample arrangements have also been made for the support of schools; in some instances council houses and churches are to be erected, dwellings constructed for the chiefs, and mills for common use. Funds have been set apart for the maintenance of the poor; the most necessary mechanical arts have been introduced, and blacksmiths, gunsmiths, wheelwrights, millwrights, etc., are supported among them. Steel and iron, and sometimes salt, are purchased for them, and plows and other farming utensils, domestic animals, looms, spinning wheels, cards, etc., are presented to them. And besides these beneficial arrangements, annuities are in all cases paid, amounting in some instances to more than $30 for each individual of the tribe, and in all cases sufficiently great, if justly divided and prudently expended, to enable them, in addition to their own exertions, to live comfortably. And as a stimulus for exertion, it is now provided by law that "in all cases of the appointment of interpreters or other persons employed for the benefit of the Indians a preference shall be given to persons of Indian descent, if such can be found who are properly qualified for the discharge of the duties."

Such are the arrangements for the physical comfort and for the moral improvement of the Indians. The necessary measures for their political advancement and for their separation from our citizens have not been neglected. The pledge of the United States has been given by Congress that the country destined for the residence of this people shall be forever "secured and guaranteed to them." A country west of Missouri and Arkansas has been assigned to them, into which the white settlements are not to be pushed. No political communities can be formed in that extensive region, except those which are established by the Indians themselves or by the United States for them and with their concurrence. A barrier has thus been raised for their protection against the encroachment of our citizens, and guarding the Indians as far as possible from those evils which have brought them to their present condition. Summary authority has been given by law to destroy all ardent spirits found in their country, without waiting the doubtful result and slow process of a legal seizure. I consider the absolute and unconditional interdiction of this article among these people as the first and great step in their melioration.

LIBERTY FOR ALL

They tell me, Liberty! that in thy name
I may not plead for all the human race;
That some are born to bondage and disgrace,
Some to a heritage of woe and shame,
And some to power supreme, and glorious fame:
With my whole soul I spurn the doctrine base,
And, as an equal brotherhood, embrace
All people, and for all fair freedom claim!
Know this, O man! whate'er thy earthly fate—
God never made a tyrant nor a slave:

Woe, then, to those who dare to desecrate
His glorious image!—for to all He gave
Eternal rights, which none may violate;
And, by a mighty hand, the oppressed He yet
    shall save!

WILLIAM LLOYD GARRISON

SENECA FALLS WOMEN'S RIGHTS
CONVENTION RESOLUTIONS

1848

Whereas, The great precept of nature is conceded to be that "man shall pursue his own true and substantial happiness." Blacktone in his *Commentaries* remarks that this law of nature being coeval with mankind, and dictated by God himself, is of course superior in obligation to any other. It is binding over all the globe, in all countries and at all times; no human laws are of any validity if contrary to this, and such of them as are valid, derive all their force, and all their validity, and all their authority, mediately and immediately, from this original; therefore,

Resolved, That all laws which prevent woman from occupying such a station in society as her conscience shall dictate, or which place her in a position inferior to that of man, are contrary to the great precept of nature, and therefore of no force or authority.

Resolved, That woman is man's equal—was intended to be so by the Creator, and the highest good of the race demands that she should be recognized as such.

Resolved, That the women of this country ought to be enlightened in regard to the laws under which they live, that they may no longer publish their degradation by declaring themselves satisfied with their present position, nor their ignorance by asserting that they have all the rights they want.

Resolved, That inasmuch as man, while claiming for himself intellectual superiority, does accord to woman moral superiority, it is preeminently his duty to encourage her to speak and teach, as she has an opportunity, in all religious assemblies.

Resolved, That the same amount of virtue, delicacy, and refinement of behavior that is required of woman in the social state, should also be required of man, and the same transgressions should be visited with equal severity on both man and woman.

Resolved, That the objection of indelicacy and impropriety, which is so often brought against woman when she addresses a public audience, comes with a very ill-grace from those who encourage, by their attendance, her appearance on the stage, in the concert, or in feats of the circus.

Resolved, That woman has too long rested satisfied in the circumscribed limits which corrupt customs and a perverted application of the Scriptures have marked out for her, and that it is time she should move in the enlarged sphere which her great Creator has assigned her.

Resolved, That it is the duty of the women of this country to secure to themselves their sacred right to the elective franchise.

Resolved, That the equality of human rights results necessarily from the fact of the identity of the race in capabilities and responsibilities.

Resolved, That the speedy success of our cause depends upon the zealous and untiring efforts of both men and women, for the overthrow of the monopoly of the pulpit, and for the securing to women an equal participation with men in the various trades, professions, and commerce.

Resolved, therefore, That, being invested by the Creator with the same capabilities, and the same consciousness of responsibility for their exercise, it is demonstrably the right and duty of woman, equally with man, to promote every righteous cause by every righteous means; and especially in regard to the great subjects of morals and religion, it is self-evidently her right to participate with her brother in teaching them, both in private and in public, by writing and by speaking, by any instrumentalities proper to be used, and in any assemblies proper to be held; and this being a self-evident truth growing out of the divinely implanted principles of human nature, any custom or authority adverse to it, whether modern or wearing the hoary sanction of antiquity, is to be regarded as a self-evident falsehood, and at war with mankind.

THE THIRTEENTH AMENDMENT TO THE CONSTITUTION: ABOLITION OF SLAVERY

Adopted December 18, 1865

SECTION 1. Neither slavery nor involuntary servitude, except as a punishment for crime whereof the party shall have been duly convicted, shall exist within the United States, or any place subject to their jurisdiction.

SECTION 2. Congress shall have power to enforce this article by appropriate legislation.

LAUS DEO!

On Hearing the Bells Ring on the Passage of the
Constitutional Amendment Abolishing Slavery,
December 18, 1865

It is done!
Clang of bell and roar of gun
Send the tidings up and down.
How the belfries rock and reel!
How the great guns, peal on peal,
Fling the joy from town to town!

Ring, O bells!
Every stroke exulting tells
Of the burial hour of crime.
Loud and long, that all may hear,
Ring for every listening ear
Of eternity and time!

Let us kneel:
God's own voice is in that peal,
And this spot is holy ground.
Lord, forgive us! What are we,
That our eyes this glory see,
That our ears have heard the sound!

For the Lord
On the whirlwind is abroad;
In the earthquake He has spoken;
He has smitten with His thunder
The iron walls asunder,
And the gates of brass are broken!

Loud and long
Lift the old exulting song;
Sing with Miriam by the sea,
He has cast the mighty down;
Horse and rider sink and drown;
"He hath triumphed gloriously!"

Did we dare,
In our agony of prayer,
Ask for more than He has done?
When was ever His right hand
Over any time or land
Stretched as now beneath the sun?

How they pale,
Ancient myth and song and tale,
In this wonder of our days,
When the cruel rod of war
Blossoms white with righteous law,
And the wrath of man is praise!

Blotted out!
All within and all about
Shall a fresher life begin;
Freer breathe the universe
As it rolls its heavy curse
On the dead and buried sin!

It is done!
In the circuit of the sun
Shall the sound thereof go forth.
It shall bid the sad rejoice,
It shall give the dumb a voice,
It shall belt with joy the earth!

Ring and swing,
Bells of joy! On morning's wing
Send the song of praise abroad!
With a sound of broken chains
Tell the nations that He reigns,
Who alone is Lord and God!

JOHN GREENLEAF WHITTIER

THE FOURTEENTH AMENDMENT TO THE CONSTITUTION: CIVIL RIGHTS

Adopted July 28, 1868

SECTION 1. All persons born or naturalized in the United States, and subject to the jurisdiction thereof, are citizens of the United States and of the state wherein they reside. No state shall make or enforce any law which shall abridge the privileges or immunities of citizens of the United States; nor shall any state deprive any person of life, liberty, or property, without due process of law; nor deny to any person within its jurisdiction the equal protection of the laws.

SECTION 2. Representatives shall be apportioned among the several states according to their respective numbers, counting the whole number of persons in each state, excluding Indians not taxed. But when the right to vote at any election for the choice of electors for president and vice president of the United States, representatives in Congress, the executive and judicial officers of a state, or the members of the legislature thereof, is denied to any of the male inhabitants of such state, being twenty-one years of age, and citizens of the United States, or in any way abridged, except for participation in rebellion, or other crime, the basis of representation therein shall be reduced in the proportion which the number of such male citizens shall bear to the whole number of male citizens twenty-one years of age in such state.

SECTION 3. No person shall be a senator or representative in Congress, or elector of president and vice president, or hold any office, civil or military, under the United States, or under any state, who, having previously taken an oath, as a member of Congress, or as an officer of the United States, or as a member of any state legislature, or as an executive or judicial officer of any state, to support the Constitution of the United States, shall have engaged in insurrection or rebellion against the same, or given aid or comfort to the enemies thereof. But Congress may by a vote of two-thirds of each House, remove such disability.

SECTION 4. The validity of the public debt of the United States, authorized by law, including debts incurred for payment of pensions and bounties for services in suppressing insurrection or rebellion, shall not be questioned. But neither the United States nor any state shall assume or pay any debt or obligation incurred in aid of insurrection or rebellion against the United States, or any claim for the loss or emancipation of any slave; but all such debts, obligations and claims shall be held illegal and void.

SECTION 5. The Congress shall have power to enforce, by appropriate legislation, the provisions of this article.

NATIVE-AMERICAN POLICY

*President Chester A. Arthur's First Annual Message
to Congress, December 6, 1881*

Prominent among the matters which challenge the attention of
Congress at its present session is the management of our Indian
affairs. While this question has been a cause of trouble and
embarrassment from the infancy of the government, it is but
recently that any effort has been made for its solution at once
serious, determined, consistent, and promising success. . . .

It was natural, at a time when the national territory seemed
almost illimitable and contained many millions of acres far
outside the bounds of civilized settlements, that a policy should
have been initiated which more than aught else has been the
fruitful source of our Indian complications.

I refer, of course, to the policy of dealing with the various
Indian tribes as separate nationalities, of relegating them by
treaty stipulations to the occupancy of immense reservations in
the West, and of encouraging them to live a savage life, undis-
turbed by any earnest and well-directed efforts to bring them
under the influences of civilization.

The unsatisfactory results which have sprung from this policy are becoming apparent to all.

As the white settlements have crowded the borders of the
reservations, the Indians, sometimes contentedly and sometimes
against their will, have been transferred to other hunting
grounds, from which they have again been dislodged whenever
their newfound homes have been desired by the adventurous
settlers.

These removals and the frontier collisions by which they
have often been preceded have led to frequent and disastrous
conflicts between the races.

It is profitless to discuss here which of them has been chiefly responsible for the disturbances whose recital occupies so large a space upon the pages of our history.

We have to deal with the appalling fact that though thousands of lives have been sacrificed and hundreds of millions of dollars expended in the attempt to solve the Indian problem, it has until within the past few years seemed scarcely nearer a solution than it was half a century ago. But the government has of late been cautiously but steadily feeling its way to the adoption of a policy which has already produced gratifying results, and which, in my judgment, is likely, if Congress and the executive accord in its support, to relieve us ere long from the difficulties which have hitherto beset us.

For the success of the efforts now making to introduce among the Indians the customs and pursuits of civilized life and gradually to absorb them into the mass of our citizens, sharing their rights and holden to their responsibilities, there is imperative need for legislative action.

My suggestions in that regard will be chiefly such as have been already called to the attention of Congress and have received to some extent its consideration.

First: I recommend the passage of an act making the laws of the various states and territories applicable to the Indian reservations within their borders and extending the laws of the state of Arkansas to the portion of the Indian Territory not occupied by the Five Civilized Tribes.

The Indian should receive the protection of the law. He should be allowed to maintain in court his rights of person and property. He has repeatedly begged for this privilege. Its exercise would be very valuable to him in his progress toward civilization.

Second: Of even greater importance is a measure which has been frequently recommended by my predecessors in office, and in furtherance of which several bills have been from time to time introduced in both Houses of Congress. The enactment of a general law permitting the allotment in severalty, to such

Indians, at least, as desire it, of a reasonable quantity of land secured to them by patent, and for their own protection made inalienable for twenty or twenty-five years, is demanded for their present welfare and their permanent advancement.

In return for such considerate action on the part of the government, there is reason to believe that the Indians in large numbers would be persuaded to sever their tribal relations and to engage at once in agricultural pursuits. Many of them realize the fact that their hunting days are over and that it is now for their best interests to conform their manner of life to the new order of things. By no greater inducement than the assurance of permanent title to the soil can they be led to engage in the occupation of tilling it.

Third: I advise a liberal appropriation for the support of Indian schools, because of my confident belief that such a course is consistent with the wisest economy.

WOMEN'S CHRISTIAN TEMPERANCE UNION DECLARATION OF PRINCIPLES

1902

We believe in the coming of His Kingdom whose service is perfect freedom, because His laws, written in our members as well as in nature and in grace, are perfect, converting the soul.

We believe in the gospel of the Golden Rule, and that each man's habits of life should be an example safe and beneficent for every other man to follow.

We believe that God created both man and woman in His own image, and therefore, we believe in one standard of purity for both men and women, and in the equal right of all to hold opinions and to express the same with equal freedom.

We believe in a living wage; in an eight-hour day; in courts of conciliation and arbitration; in justice as opposed to greed of gain; in "peace on earth and good will to men."

We therefore formulate, and for ourselves adopt the following pledge, asking our sisters and brothers of a common danger and a common hope, to make common cause with us, in working its reasonable and helpful precepts into the practice of everyday life:

I hereby solemnly promise *God helping me,* to abstain from all distilled, fermented, and malt liquors, including wine, beer, and cider, and to employ all proper means to discourage the use of and traffic in the same.

To conform and enforce the rationale of this pledge, we declare our purpose to educate the young; to form a better public sentiment; to reform so far as possible, by religious, ethical, and scientific means, the drinking classes; to seek the transforming power of divine grace for ourselves and all for whom we work, that they and we may willfully transcend no law of pure and wholesome living; and finally we pledge ourselves to labor and to pray that all of these principles, founded upon the gospel of Christ, may be worked out into the customs of society and the laws of the land.

THE MAN WITH THE MUCK-RAKE

Over a century ago Washington laid the cornerstone of the Capitol in what was then little more than a tract of wooded wilderness here beside the Potomac. We now find it necessary to provide by great additional buildings for the business of the government. This growth in the need for the housing of the government is but a proof and example of the way in which the nation has grown and the sphere of action of the national government has grown. We now administer the affairs of a nation in which the extraordinary growth of population has been outstripped by the growth of wealth and the growth in complex interests. The material problems that face us today are not such as they were in Washington's time, but the underlying facts of human nature are the same now as they were then. Under altered external form we war with the same tendencies toward evil that were evident in Washington's time, and are helped by the same tendencies for good. It is about some of these that I wish to say a word today.

In Bunyan's *Pilgrim's Progress* you may recall the description of the Man with the Muck-Rake, the man who could look no way but downward, with the muck-rake in his hand; who was offered a celestial crown for his muck-rake, but who would neither look up nor regard the crown he was offered, but continued to rake to himself the filth of the floor.

In *Pilgrim's Progress* the Man with the Muck-Rake is set forth as the example of him whose vision is fixed on carnal instead of on spiritual things. Yet he also typifies the man who in this life consistently refuses to see aught that is lofty and fixes his eyes with solemn intentness only on that which is vile and debasing. Now, it is very necessary that we should not flinch from seeing what is vile and debasing. There is filth on the floor, and it must be scraped up with the muck-rake: and there are times and places where this service is the most needed of all the services that can be performed. But the man who never does

191

anything else, who never thinks or speaks or writes save of his feats with the muck-rake, speedily becomes, not a help to society, not an incitement to good, but one of the most potent forces for evil.

There are, in the body politic, economic, and social, many and grave evils, and there is urgent necessity for the sternest war upon them. There should be relentless exposure of and attack upon every evil man, whether politician or business man, every evil practice, whether in politics, in business, or in social life. I hail as a benefactor every writer or speaker, every man who, on the platform, or in book, magazine, or newspaper, with merciless severity makes such attack, provided always that he in his turn remembers that the attack is of use only if it is absolutely truthful. The liar is no whit better than the thief, and if his mendacity takes the form of slander, he may be worse than most thieves. It puts a premium upon knavery untruthfully to attack an honest man, or even with hysterical exaggeration to assail a bad man with untruth. An epidemic of indiscriminate assault upon character does no good but very great harm. . . .

My plea is not for immunity to but for the most unsparing exposure of the politician who betrays his trust, of the big-business man who makes or spends his fortune in illegitimate or corrupt ways. There should be a resolute effort to hunt every such man out of the position he has disgraced. Expose the crime, and hunt down the criminal; but remember that even in the case of crime, if it is attacked in sensational, lurid, and untruthful fashion, the attack may do more damage to the public mind than the crime itself. It is because I feel that there should be no rest in the endless war against the forces of evil that I ask that the war be conducted with sanity as well as with resolution. The men with the muck-rakes are often indispensable to the well-being of society; but only if they know when to stop raking the muck, and to look upward to the celestial crown above them, to the crown of worthy endeavor. There are beautiful things above and round about them; and if they gradually grow to feel that the whole world is nothing but muck, their power of usefulness is gone. If the whole picture is painted black, there remains no hue whereby to single out the rascals for distinction from their fellows. Such painting finally induces a kind of moral color-blindness; and people affected by it come to the conclusion that no man is really black, and no man really white, but that all are gray. . . .

To assail the great and admitted evils of our political and industrial life with such crude and sweeping generalizations as to include decent men in the general condemnation means the searing of the public conscience. There results a general attitude either of cynical belief in and indifference to public corruption or else of a distrustful inability to discriminate between the good and the bad. Either attitude is fraught with untold damage to the country as a whole. The fool who has not sense to discriminate between what is good and what is bad is well-nigh as dangerous as the man who does discriminate and yet chooses the bad. There is nothing more distressing to every good patriot, to every good American, than the hard, scoffing spirit which treats the allegation of dishonesty in a public man as a cause for laughter. . . .

There is any amount of good in the world, and there never was a time when loftier and more disinterested work for the betterment of mankind was being done than now. The forces that tend for evil are great and terrible but the forces of truth and love and courage and honesty and generosity and sympathy are also stronger than ever before. It is a foolish and timid, no less than a wicked, thing to blink the fact that the forces of evil are strong, but it is even worse to fail to take into account the strength of the forces that tell for good. Hysterical sensationalism is the very poorest weapon wherewith to fight for lasting righteousness. The men who, with stern sobriety and truth, assail the many evils of our time, whether in the public press, or in magazines, or in books, are the leaders and allies of all engaged in the work for social and political betterment. But if they give good reason for distrust of what they say, if they chill the ardor of those who demand truth as a primary virtue, they thereby betray the good cause, and play into the hands of the very men against whom they are nominally at war. . . .

We can no more and no less afford to condone evil in the man of capital than evil in the man of no capital. The wealthy man who exults because there is a failure of justice in the effort to bring some trust magnate to an account for his misdeeds is as bad as, and no worse than, the so-called labor leader who clamorously strives to excite a foul class feeling on behalf of some other labor leader who is implicated in murder. One attitude is as bad as the other and no worse; in each case the accused is entitled to exact justice; and in neither case is there need of action by others which can be construed into an expression of sympathy for crime. There is nothing more antisocial in a democratic republic like ours than such vicious class-consciousness. . . .

It is important to this people to grapple with the problems connected with the amassing of enormous fortunes, and the use of those fortunes, both corporate and individual, in business. We should discriminate in the sharpest way between fortunes well won and fortunes ill won; between those gained as an incident to performing great services to the community as a whole, and those gained in evil fashion by keeping just within the limits of mere law-honesty. Of course no amount of charity in spending such fortunes in any way compensates for misconduct in making them. As a matter of personal conviction, and without pretending to discuss the details or formulate the system, I feel that we shall ultimately have to consider the adoption of some such scheme as that of a progressive tax on all fortunes, beyond a certain amount, either given in life or devised or bequeathed upon death to any individual—a tax so framed as to put it out of the power of the owner of one of these enormous fortunes to hand on more than a certain amount to any one individual. . . .

The eighth commandment reads "Thou shalt not steal." It does not read "Thou shalt not steal from the rich man." It does not read "Thou shalt not steal from the poor man." It reads, simply and plainly, "Thou shalt not steal." No good whatever will come from that warped and mock morality which denounces the misdeeds of men of wealth and forgets the misdeeds practiced at their expense; which denounces bribery, but blinds itself to blackmail; which foams with rage if a corporation secures favors by improper methods, and merely leers with hideous mirth if the corporation is itself wronged. The only public servant who can be trusted honestly to protect the rights of the public against the misdeeds of a corporation is that public man who will just as surely protect the corporation itself from wrongful aggression. If a public man is willing to yield to popular clamor and do wrong to the men of wealth or to rich corporations, it may be set down as certain that if the opportunity comes he will secretly and furtively do wrong to the public in the interest of a corporation. . . .

More important than aught else is the development of the broadest sympathy of man for man. The welfare of the wage-worker, the welfare of the tiller of the soil—upon this depends the welfare of the entire country; their good is not to be sought in pulling down others; but their good must be the prime object of all our statesmanship.

Materially we must strive to secure a broader economic opportunity for all men, so that each shall have a better chance to show the stuff of which he is made. Spiritually and ethically we must strive to bring about clean living and right thinking. We appreciate that the things of the body are important; but we appreciate also that the things of the soul are immeasurably more important. The foundation stone of national life is, and ever must be, the high individual character of the average citizen.

President Theodore Roosevelt,
from a speech at the House of Representatives,
Washington, D.C., April 14, 1906

The Nineteenth Amendment
to the Constitution:
Women's Suffrage

Adopted August 26, 1920

SECTION 1. The right of citizens of the United States to vote shall not be denied or abridged by the United States or by any state on account of sex.

SECTION 2. Congress shall have power to enforce this article by appropriate legislation.

Religious Tolerance

There is in Mexico undoubtedly a condition, a lamentable condition; there is unquestionably brutal mistreatment not only of the Catholic church but, I think, of all other churches that have established themselves there; but that is a question for Mexico. It is not for us. I think that is the sentiment in the hearts of the great Catholic population of this country, as it is of the non-Catholic population. There may be here and there a Catholic who takes an extreme view, as I believe if any Protestant denomination found the brethren of its faith being persecuted there would also be some of them who would take an extreme view. These things are natural; but if they exist in sporadic instances no general indictment of the Catholic church is thereby justified; no attempt should be made to arouse prejudice against these good citizens. There has been much of that kind of appeal made in the last few years. It is a shameful appeal, by whomsoever made or wherever made. It is not a new thing. It has broken out periodically throughout the entire story of our national life.

Mr. President, I do not know that we shall gain anything by prolonging a discussion of this kind. I am sorry it has occurred. So that I may remove all taint of suspicion that I speak from interested motives, I remark that I was born and reared in the Presbyterian faith; that my ancestors signed the original covenant of the Protestants of Great Britain; and that I have not a relative on earth that I know of who is not of the Protestant faith. Neither, sir, am I a member of the Ku Klux Klan; I hope if there be a little remnant of loyalty left that is not completely absorbed, a little love of country that does not all emanate form and repose in a single breast, that in common with the other members of this body I may be credited with at least a small degree of patriotism.

I have friends of the Catholic faith; I know many priests of the Catholic church; I know three or four bishops and one or two archbishops; and I join the senator from Maryland in the statement that no living Catholic has ever appealed to me to raise a religious dispute, to seek to stir up animosity, or to provoke war with Mexico.

A Catholic signed the Declaration of Independence along with Protestants. Catholic and Protestant, Jew and Gentile, marshaled under the banners of George Washington. Catholic and Protestant, Jew and Gentile, died on every field of the Revolution.

Catholic and Protestant, Jew and Gentile, manned the ships of 1812, fought throughout the war, touched elbows behind the cotton bales at New Orleans, and mingled their blood in one common stream that victory might glorify American arms.

Catholic and Protestant, Jew and Gentile, bore our flag across the plains of Mexico and planted it in glory above the castles of the Montezumas.

Catholic and Protestant, Jew and Gentile, in the fratracidal war of 1861 rallied to the standard of the South and rallied to the banner of the North, according to the sectional lines that divided them, and with equal gallantry and courage laid down their lives upon the gory fields of that awful struggle.

And, sir, when the war with Spain came, Catholic and Protestant, Jew and Gentile, rushed to the colors and charged to death amidst a storm of Spanish bullets. On all these gory fields the Protestant nurse and the Catholic sister alike ministered to the dying and cared for the wounded. Bending above the bodies of soldiers whose souls were departing was the Catholic priest with his cross and likewise the Protestant minister with his Bible.

Then came the last Great War. We saw the soldiers as they were called from farm and factory, from office and university, from cabin and from palace. They did not come, sir, as Catholics or Protestants, as Jews or Gentiles, they came as American citizens.

They marched away with the same manly stride, with the same gleam of courage in their eyes, the same hot flame of patriotism burning in their hearts—Jew and Gentile, Catholic and Protestant. On the gory plains of France they fought and died together—Jew and Gentile, Catholic and Protestant. Amidst the storm of shot and shell, through fogs of deadly gases, Catholic boys bore from the field the torn bodies of Protestant comrades, and Protestant boys with equal fortitude gathered the helpless bodies of Catholic boys in their arms and carried them to safety.

In camp and field, in trench and hospital, the Young Men's Christian Association, the Salvation Army, the Knights of Columbus, and the Jewish societies labored in cooperation to ameliorate suffering, to assuage pain. Catholic priests and Catholic nuns, Jewish rabbis and Jewish nurses, Protestant clergymen and Protestant nurses, together with physicians of all religions and of no religion, with equal tenderness and heroism alleviated the hardships of the field and the agonies of the hospital.

There came the day of peace. The brown columns began the

return march. The gold-star mothers gathered to gaze at the gaps once filled by their gallant dead. So they stood, Jewish mothers and Gentile mothers, Catholic mothers and Protestant mothers—the same pain in their heart, the same tear in their eye. The gallant survivors heard the silvery music of welcoming bands; the cheers of mighty multitudes that rose and broke like the waves of a vast ocean—cheers for the soldiers of liberty. In that moment the returning heroes found some compensation for their sacrifices. Their bosoms thrilled with pride that they had helped to save and sanctify our flag, every star of which proclaims liberty for all, equality for all, justice for all, the right to worship God according to the dictates of conscience.

They were mustered out. Yet they had scarce turned their faces toward their homes until the Catholic soldier heard the serpent hiss of proscription and saw men massing who proposed to proscribe and persecute him because he worshiped God according to the tenets of his church.

If my country means anything to me, sir, it means that its Constitution is broad enough to protect every man in the right to his faith, every man in the right to his opinion, every man in his liberty of speech, in the right of peaceable assemblage, and in his privilege to print his honest thoughts.

If this country is to live, then these fountain springs bearing the pure waters of liberty must not be polluted with the poison of hate, covered with the slime of proscription, or polluted by the spirit of intolerance. Intolerance, sir, is the child of ignorance. Give me the radius of any man's intelligence, and I will describe the circumference of his tolerance.

It is useless for the senator from Alabama to shout, "I do not bring in religion." He has brought in the question of religion; he has thrice brought it in.

No good purpose is to be served. No informed person believes that the great body of our Catholic people are trying to drive us into a war with Mexico on account of religion.

I do not want to make this a personal matter. All I desire to say is that religion itself condemns these persecutions. The spirit of religion, of real religion, is that of tolerance. Bigotry has no place beneath the spire of a Protestant tabernacle, under the cross of a Catholic church, or within the walls of a Jewish synagogue.

Tolerance and good will, charity and kindliness—these are the four angles that encompass the temples of real religion. We ought to have some of it everywhere and always.

This much I desire to say, that if it were for me to decide, I would do as we did when there was persecution of the people in Ireland. I would use the good offices of the government to stop persecution in Mexico. I would equally do so were the persecution directed against the Protestant churches of Mexico; I would do so even if a portion of the Mexican people were being oppressed and slaughtered. Scores and scores of times our government has protested against wrongs and cruelties in foreign lands. Scores of times we have expressed sympathy for the unfortunate. Scores of times we have tendered our good offices without danger of war and to the credit of Christian civilization.

Mr. President, I may have angered my friend; I do not want to. I merely say that when we are forced to discuss religious questions in the Senate, he who begins the discussion must accept the responsibility. They were not here until the senator from Alabama spoke. Of course, he has the right to protest against war. We all can protest against war. We are all against war. But against the ground of his opposition I protest and object.

In conclusion, permit me to issue this warning: War may be produced by improvident acts and foolish agitation. Incendiary editorials and inflammatory speeches made in this country will be repeated in Mexican papers and accompanied by like recriminations. The Mexican articles may then be reprinted in the United States, accompanied by still more denunciatory utterances. So the process of stirring up hatred, suspicion, and fear may be carried to such a degree as to produce a demand for war.

More than one great war has been caused by similar processes. At such a time as this, patience, forbearance, and calm councils, accompanied by a spirit of fairness, ought to prevail. Such a course will in all probability avoid any serious trouble with the Republic of Mexico. An opposite course is full of menace.

Senator James A. Reed,
from a speech before the U.S. Senate, 1927

The Constitution of the American Federation of Labor

1932

PREAMBLE

Whereas, A struggle is going on in all the nations of the civilized world between the oppressors and the oppressed of all countries, a struggle between the capitalist and the laborer, which grows in intensity from year to year, and will work disastrous results to the toiling millions if they are not combined for mutual protection and benefit. It, therefore, behooves the representatives of the trade and labor unions of America, in convention assembled, to adopt such measures and disseminate such principles among the mechanics and laborers of our country as will permanently unite them to secure the recognition of rights to which they are justly entitled. We, therefore, declare ourselves in favor of the formation of thorough federation, embracing every trade and labor organization in America, organized under the trade union system.

ARTICLE I: NAME

This association shall be known as the American Federation of Labor, and shall consist of such trade and labor unions as shall conform to its rules and regulations.

ARTICLE II: OBJECTS

SECTION 1. The object of this federation shall be the encouragement and formation of local trade and labor unions, and the closer federation of such societies through the organization of central trade and labor unions in every city, and the further combination of such bodies into state, territorial, or provincial organizations to secure legislation in the interest of the working masses.

SECTION 2. The establishment of national and international trade unions, based upon a strict recognition of the autonomy of each trade, and the promotion and advancement of such bodies.

SECTION 3. The establishment of departments composed of national or international unions affiliated with the American Federation of Labor, of the same industry, and which departments shall be governed in conformity with the laws of the American Federation of Labor.

SECTION 4. An American federation of all national and international trade unions, to aid and assist each other; to aid and encourage the sale of union label goods, and to secure legislation in the interest of the working people, and influence public opinion, by peaceful and legal methods, in favor of organized labor.

SECTION 5. To aid and encourage the labor press of America. . . .

SECTION 8. Party politics, whether they be Democratic, Republican, Socialist, Populistic, Prohibition, or any other, shall have no place in the conventions of the American Federation of Labor. . . .

ARTICLE IX: EXECUTIVE COUNCIL

SECTION 1. It shall be the duty of the Executive Council to watch legislative measures directly affecting the interests of working people, and to initiate, whenever necessary, such legislative action as the convention may direct.

SECTION 2. The Executive Council shall use every possible means to organize new national or international trade or labor unions, and to organize local trade and labor unions, and connect them with the federation until such time as there is a sufficient number to form a national or international union, when it shall be the duty of the president of the federation to see that such organization is formed. . . .

ARTICLE X: REVENUE

SECTION 1. The revenue of the federation shall be derived from a per capita tax to be paid upon the full paid-up membership of all affiliated bodies. . . .

ARTICLE XI: LOCAL CENTRAL BODIES . . .

SECTION 2. It shall be the duty of all national and international unions affiliated with the American Federation of Labor to instruct their local unions to join chartered central labor bodies, departments, and state federations in their vicinity where such exist. Similar instructions shall be given by the American Federation of Labor to all trade and federal labor unions under its jurisdiction. . . .

SECTION 5. No central labor union, or other central body of delegates, shall have the authority or power to order any organization, affiliated with such central labor union, or other central labor body, on strike, or to take a strike vote, where such organization has a national organization, until the proper authorities of such national or international organization have been consulted and agreed to such action. . . .

SECTION 7. No central labor union, or other central body of delegates, shall have authority or power to originate a boycott, nor shall such bodies indorse and order the placing of the name of any person, firm, or corporation on an unfair list until the local union desiring the same has, before declaring the boycott, submitted the matter in dispute to the central body for investigation, and the best endeavors on its part to effect an amicable settlement. Violation of this section shall forfeit charter. . . .

ARTICLE XII: ASSESSMENT IN DEFENSE OF NATIONAL AND INTERNATIONAL UNIONS

SECTION 1. The Executive Council shall have power to declare a levy of one cent per member per week on all affiliated unions for a period not exceeding ten weeks in any one year, to assist in the support of an affiliated national or international union engaged in a protracted strike or lockout. . . .

ARTICLE XIII: DEFENSE FUND FOR LOCAL TRADE AND FEDERAL LABOR UNIONS

SECTION 1. Unless otherwise ordered by the Executive Council the moneys of the defense fund shall be drawn only to sustain strikes or lockouts of local trade and federal labor unions when such strikes or lockouts are authorized, endorsed, and conducted in conformity with the following provisions of this article: . . .

SECTION 7. Any union inaugurating a strike without the approval of the Executive Council shall not receive benefit on account of said strike. . . .

SECTION 10. Before a strike shall be declared off, a special meeting of the union shall be called for that purpose, and it shall require a majority vote of all members present to decide the question either way.

THE NATIONAL RECOVERY ACT

June 16, 1933

TITLE I: INDUSTRIAL RECOVERY

DECLARATION OF POLICY, SECTION 1. A national emergency productive of widespread unemployment and disorganization of industry, which burdens interstate and foreign commerce, affects the public welfare, and undermines the standards of living of the American people, is hereby declared to exist. It is hereby declared to be the policy of Congress to remove obstructions to the free flow of interstate and foreign commerce which tend to diminish the amount thereof; and to provide for the general welfare by promoting the organization of industry for the purpose of cooperative action among trade groups, to induce and maintain united action of labor and management under adequate governmental sanctions and supervision, to eliminate unfair competitive practices, to promote the fullest possible utilization of the present productive capacity of industries, to avoid undue restriction of production (except as may be temporarily required), to increase the consumption of industrial and agricultural products by increasing purchasing power, to reduce and relieve unemployment, to improve standards of labor, and otherwise to rehabilitate industry and to conserve natural resources. . . .

AGREEMENTS AND LICENSES, SECTION 4. (a) The president is authorized to enter into agreements with, and to approve voluntary agreements between and among, persons engaged in a trade or industry, labor organizations, and trade or industrial organizations, associations, or groups, relating to any trade or industry, if in his judgment such agreements will aid in effectuating the policy of this title with respect to transactions in or affecting interstate or foreign commerce. . . .

(b) Whenever the president shall find that destructive wage or price cutting or other activities contrary to the policy of this title are being practiced in any trade or industry or any subdivision thereof, and, after such public notice and hearing as he shall specify, shall find it essential to license business enterprises in order to make effective a code of fair competition or an agreement under this title or otherwise to effectuate the policy of this title, and shall publicly so announce, no person shall, after a date fixed in such announcement, engage in or carry on any business, in or affecting interstate or foreign commerce, specified in such announcement, unless he shall have first obtained a license issued pursuant to such regulations as the president shall prescribe. . . .

TITLE II: PUBLIC WORKS AND CONSTRUCTION PROJECTS

FEDERAL EMERGENCY ADMINISTRATION OF PUBLIC WORKS, SECTION 201. (a) To effectuate the purposes of this title, the president is hereby authorized to create a Federal Emergency Administration of Public Works, all the powers of which shall be exercised by a Federal Emergency Administrator of Public Works. . . .

SECTION 202. The administrator, under the direction of the president, shall prepare a comprehensive program of public works, which shall include among other things the following: (a) construction, repair, and improvement of public highways and park ways, public buildings, and any publicly owned instrumentalities and facilities; (b) conservation and development of natural resources, including control, utilization, and purification of waters, prevention of soil or coastal erosion, development of water power, transmission of electrical energy, and construction of river and harbor improvements and flood control. . . .

SECTION 203. (a) With a view to increasing employment quickly (while reasonably securing any loans made by the United States), the president is authorized and empowered, through the administrator or through such other agencies as he may designate or create, (1) to construct, finance, or aid in the construction or financing of any public-works project included in the program prepared pursuant to Section 202; (2) upon such terms as the president shall prescribe, to make grants to states, municipalities, or other public bodies for the construction, repair, or improvement of any such project, but no such grant shall be in excess of 30 percentum of the cost of the labor and materials employed upon such project; (3) to acquire by purchase, or by exercise of the power of eminent domain, any real or personal property in connection with the construction of any such project, and to sell any security acquired or any property so constructed or acquired or to lease any such property with or without the privilege of purchase; . . . (4) to aid in the financing of such railroad maintenance and equipment as may be approved by the Interstate Commerce Commission as desirable for the improvement of transportation facilities. . . .

SECTION 204. (a) For the purpose of providing for emergency construction of public highways and related projects, the president is authorized to make grants to the highway departments of the several states in an amount not less than $400 million, to be expended by such departments in accordance with the provisions of the Federal Highway Act. . . .

SECTION 205. (a) Not less than $50 million of the amount made available by this act shall be allotted for (A) national forest highways, (B) national forest roads, trails, bridges, and related projects, (C) national park roads and trails in national parks owned or authorized, (D) roads on Indian reservations, and (E) roads through public lands. . . .

SUBSISTENCE HOMESTEADS, SECTION 208. To provide for aiding the redistribution of the overbalance of population in industrial centers $25 million is hereby made available to the president, to be used by him through such agencies as he may establish and under such regulations as he may make, for making loans for and otherwise aiding in the purchase of subsistence homesteads.

THE SOCIAL SECURITY ACT

*President Franklin Delano Roosevelt's Statement
on Signing the Act, August 14, 1935*

Today a hope of many years standing is in large part fulfilled. The civilization of the past hundred years, with its startling industrial changes, has tended more and more to make life insecure. Young people have come to wonder what would be their lot when they came to old age. The man with a job has wondered how long the job would last.

This social security measure gives at least some protection to thirty million of our citizens who will reap direct benefits through unemployment compensation, through old-age pensions, and through increased services for the protection of children and the prevention of ill health.

We can never insure 100 percent of the population against 100 percent of the hazards and vicissitudes of life, but we have tried to frame a law which will give some measure of protection to the average citizen and to his family against the loss of a job and against poverty-ridden old age.

This law, too, represents a cornerstone in a structure which is being built but is by no means complete—a structure intended to lessen the force of possible future depressions, to act as a protection to future administrations of the government against the necessity of going deeply into debt to furnish relief to the needy—a law to flatten out the peaks and valleys of deflation and of inflation—in other words, a law that will take care of human needs and at the same time provide for the United States an economic structure of vastly greater soundness.

I congratulate all of you ladies and gentlemen, all of you in the Congress, in the executive departments and all of you who come from private life, and I thank you for your splendid efforts in behalf of this sound, needy, and patriotic legislation.

If the Senate and the House of Representatives in this long and arduous session had done nothing more than pass this bill, the session would be regarded as historic for all time.

Civil Rights Policy

President Harry S. Truman's Message to Congress, February 2, 1948

In the state-of-the-union message on January 7, 1948, I spoke of five great goals toward which we should strive in our constant effort to strengthen our democracy and improve the welfare of our people. The first of these is to secure fully our essential human rights. I am now presenting to the Congress my recommendations for legislation to carry us forward toward that goal.

This nation was founded by men and women who sought these shores that they might enjoy greater freedom and greater opportunity than they had known before. The founders of the United States proclaimed to the world the American belief that all men are created equal, and that governments are instituted to secure the inalienable rights with which all men are endowed. In the Declaration of Independence and the Constitution of the United States they eloquently expressed the aspirations of all mankind for equality and freedom.

These ideals inspired the peoples of other lands, and their practical fulfillment made the United States the hope of the oppressed everywhere. Throughout our history men and women of all colors and creeds, of all races and religions, have come to this country to escape tyranny and discrimination. Millions strong, they have helped build this democratic nation and have constantly reinforced our devotion to the great ideals of liberty and equality. With those who preceded them, they have helped to fashion and strengthen our American faith—a faith that can be simply stated:

We believe that all men are created equal and that they have the right to equal justice under law.

We believe that all men have the right to freedom of thought and of expression and the right to worship as they please.

We believe that all men are entitled to equal opportunities for jobs, for homes, for good health, and for education.

We believe that all men should have a voice in their government, and that government should protect, not usurp, the rights of the people.

These are the basic civil rights which are the source and the support of our democracy.

Today the American people enjoy more freedom and opportunity than ever before. Never in our history has there been better reason to hope for the complete realization of the ideals of liberty and equality.

We shall not, however, finally achieve the ideals for which this nation was founded so long as any American suffers discrimination as a result of his race, or religion, or color, or the land of origin of his forefathers.

Unfortunately there still are examples—flagrant examples—of discrimination which are utterly contrary to our ideals. Not all groups of our population are free from the fear of violence. Not all groups are free to live and work where they please or to improve their conditions of life by their own efforts.

Not all groups enjoy the full privileges of citizenship and participation in the government under which they live.

We cannot be satisfied until all our people have equal opportunities for jobs, for homes, for education, for health, and for political expression, and until all our people have equal protection under the law. . . .

The protection of civil rights is the duty of every government which derives its powers from the consent of the people. This is equally true of local, state, and national governments. There is much that the states can and should do at this time to extend their protection of civil rights. Wherever the law-enforcement measures of state and local governments are inadequate to discharge this primary function of government, these measures should be strengthened and improved.

The federal government has a clear duty to see that constitutional guarantees of individual liberties and of equal protection under the laws are not denied or abridged anywhere in our Union. That duty is shared by all three branches of the government, but it can be fulfilled only if the Congress enacts modern, comprehensive civil rights laws, adequate to the needs of the day, and demonstrating our continuing faith in the free way of life.

I recommend, therefore, that the Congress enact legislation at this session directed toward the following specific objectives:

1. Establishing a permanent Commission on Civil Rights, a Joint Congressional Committee on Civil Rights, and a Civil Rights Division in the Department of Justice.

2. Strengthening existing civil rights statutes.

3. Providing federal protection against lynching.

4. Protecting more adequately the right to vote.

5. Establishing a Fair Employment Practice Commission to prevent unfair discrimination in employment.

6. Prohibiting discrimination in interstate transportation facilities.

7. Providing home rule and suffrage in presidential elections for the residents of the District of Columbia.

8. Providing statehood for Hawaii and Alaska and a greater measure of self-government for our island possessions.

9. Equalizing the opportunities for residents of the United States to become naturalized citizens.

10. Settling the evacuation claims of Japanese-Americans. . . .

Under the authority of existing law the executive branch is taking every possible action to improve the enforcement of the civil rights statutes and to eliminate discrimination in federal employment, in providing federal services and facilities, and in the armed forces.

I have already referred to the establishment of the Civil Rights Division of the Department of Justice. The Federal Bureau of Investigation will work closely with this new division in the investigation of federal civil rights cases. Specialized training is being given to the bureau's agents so that they may render more effective service in this difficult field of law enforcement.

It is the settled policy of the United States government that there shall be no discrimination in federal employment or in providing federal services and facilities. Steady progress has been made toward this objective in recent years. I shall shortly issue an executive order containing a comprehensive restatement of the federal nondiscrimination policy, together with appropriate measures to ensure compliance.

During the recent war and in the years since its close we have made much progress toward equality of opportunity in our armed services without regard to race, color, religion, or national origin. I have instructed the secretary of defense to take steps to have the remaining instances of discrimination in the armed services eliminated as rapidly as possible. The personnel policies and practices of all the services in this regard will be made consistent. . . .

We in the United States are working in company with other nations who share our desire for enduring world peace and who believe with us that, above all else, men must be free. We are striving to build a world family of nations—a world where men may live under governments of their own choosing and under laws of their own making.

As part of that endeavor, the Commission on Human Rights of the United Nations is now engaged in preparing an international bill of human rights by which the nations of the world may bind themselves by international covenant to give effect to basic human rights and fundamental freedoms. We have played a leading role in this undertaking designed to create a world order of law and justice fully protective of the rights and the dignity of the individual.

To be effective in these efforts, we must protect our civil rights so that by providing all our people with the maximum enjoyment of personal freedom and personal opportunity we shall be a stronger nation—stronger in our leadership, stronger in our moral position, stronger in the deeper satisfactions of a united citizenry.

We know that our democracy is not perfect. But we do know that it offers a fuller, freer, happier life to our people than any totalitarian nation has ever offered.

If we wish to inspire the peoples of the world whose freedom is in jeopardy, if we wish to restore hope to those who have already lost their civil liberties, if we wish to fulfill the promise that is ours, we must correct the remaining imperfections in our practice of democracy.

We know the way. We need only the will.

THE TWENTY-FOURTH AMENDMENT TO THE CONSTITUTION: VOTING RIGHTS

Adopted January 23, 1964

SECTION 1. The right of citizens of the United States to vote in any primary or other election for president or vice president, for electors for president or vice president, or for senator or representative in Congress, shall not be denied or abridged by the United States or any state by reason of failure to pay any poll tax or other tax.

SECTION 2. The Congress shall have power to enforce this article by appropriate legislation.

THE PEACE CORPS

President John F. Kennedy's Message to Congress,
March 1, 1961

Throughout the world the people of the newly developing nations are struggling for economic and social progress which reflects their deepest desires. Our own freedom, and the future of freedom around the world, depend, in a very real sense, on their ability to build growing and independent nations where men can live in dignity, liberated from the bonds of hunger, ignorance, and poverty.

One of the greatest obstacles to the achievement of this goal is the lack of trained men and women with the skill to teach the young and assist in the operation of development projects—men and women with the capacity to cope with the demands of swiftly evolving economies, and with the dedication to put that capacity to work in the villages, the mountains, the towns, and the factories of dozens of struggling nations.

The vast task of economic development urgently requires skilled people to do the work of the society—to help teach in the schools, construct development projects, demonstrate modern methods of sanitation in the villages, and perform a hundred other tasks calling for training and advanced knowledge.

To meet this urgent need for skilled manpower we are proposing the establishment of a Peace Corps—an organization which will recruit and train American volunteers, sending them abroad to work with the people of other nations.

This organization will differ from existing assistance programs in that its members will supplement technical advisers by offering the specific skills needed by developing nations if they are to put technical advice to work. They will help provide the skilled manpower necessary to carry out the development projects planned by the host governments, acting at a working level and serving at great personal sacrifice. . . .

Last session, the Congress authorized a study of these possibilities. Preliminary reports of this study show that the Peace Corps is feasible, needed, and wanted by many foreign countries.

Most heartening of all, the initial reaction to this proposal has been an enthusiastic response by student groups, professional organizations, and private citizens everywhere—a convincing demonstration that we have in this country an immense reservoir of dedicated men and women willing to devote their energies and time and toil to the cause of world peace and human progress.

Among the specific programs to which Peace Corps members can contribute are teaching in primary and secondary schools, especially as part of national English language teaching programs; participation in the worldwide program of malaria eradication; instruction and operation of public health and sanitation projects; aiding in village development through school construction and other programs; increasing rural agricultural productivity by assisting local farmers to use modern implements and techniques. The initial emphasis of these programs will be on teaching. . . .

The Peace Corps will not be limited to the young, or to college graduates. All Americans who are qualified will be welcome to join this effort. But undoubtedly the corps will be made up primarily of young people as they complete their formal education.

Because one of the greatest resources of a free society is the strength and diversity of its private organizations and institutions much of the Peace Corps program will be carried out by these groups, financially assisted by the federal government.

Peace Corps personnel will be made available to developing nations in the following ways:

1. Through private voluntary agencies carrying on international assistance programs.
2. Through overseas programs of colleges and universities.
3. Through assistance programs of international agencies.
4. Through assistance programs of the U.S. government.
5. Through new programs which the Peace Corps itself directly administers.

In the majority of cases the Peace Corps will assume the entire responsibility for recruitment, training, and the development of overseas projects. In other cases it will make available a pool of trained applicants to private groups who are carrying out projects approved by the Peace Corps.

In all instances the men and women of the Peace Corps will go only to those countries where their services and skills are genuinely needed and desired. U. S. operations missions, supplemented where necessary by special Peace Corps teams, will consult with leaders in foreign countries in order to determine where Peace Corpsmen are needed, the types of job they can best fill, and the number of people who can be usefully employed. The Peace Corps will not supply personnel for marginal undertakings without a sound economic or social justification. In furnishing assistance through the Peace Corps careful regard will be given to the particular country's developmental priorities.

Membership in the Peace Corps will be open to all Americans, and applications will be available shortly. Where application is made directly to the Peace Corps—the vast majority of cases—they will be carefully screened to make sure that those who are selected can contribute to Peace Corps programs and have the personal qualities which will enable them to represent the United States abroad with honor and dignity. In those cases where application is made directly to a private group, the same basic standards will be maintained. Each new recruit will receive a training and orientation period varying from six weeks to six months. This training will include courses in the culture and language of the country to which they are being sent and specialized training designed to increase the work skills of recruits. . . .

Length of service in the corps will vary depending on the kind of project and the country, generally ranging from two to three years. Peace Corps members will often serve under conditions of physical hardship, living under primitive conditions among the people of developing nations. For every Peace Corps member service will mean a great financial sacrifice. They will receive no salary. Instead they will be given an allowance which will only be sufficient to meet their basic needs and maintain health. It is essential that Peace Corps men and women live simply and unostentatiously among the people they have come to assist. At the conclusion of their tours, members of the Peace Corps will receive a small sum in the form of severance pay based on length of service abroad to assist them during their first weeks back in the United States. Service with the Peace Corps will not exempt volunteers from selective service.

THE GREAT SOCIETY

President Lyndon Johnson's Speech at the University of Michigan, Ann Arbor, May 22, 1964

I have come today from the turmoil of your Capitol to the tranquillity of your campus to speak about the future of our country. The purpose of protecting the life of our nation and preserving the liberty of our citizens is to pursue the happiness of our people. Our success in that pursuit is the test of our success as a nation. For a century we labored to settle and to subdue a continent. For half a century, we called upon unbounded invention and untiring industry to create an order of plenty for all our people. The challenge of the next half century is whether we have the wisdom to use that wealth to enrich and elevate our national life, and to advance the quality of our American civilization.

Your imagination, your initiative, and your indignation will determine whether we build a society where progress is the servant of our needs, or a society where old values and new visions are buried under unbridled growth. For in your time we have the opportunity to move not only toward the rich society and the powerful society, but upward to the Great Society. The Great Society rests on abundance and liberty for all. It demands an end to poverty and racial injustice, to which we are totally committed in our time. But that is just the beginning. The Great Society is a place where every child can find knowledge to enrich his mind and to enlarge his talents. It is a place where leisure is a welcome chance to build and reflect, not a feared cause of boredom and restlessness. It is a place where the city of man serves not only the needs of the body and the demands of commerce, but the desire for beauty and the hunger for community.

It is a place where man can renew contact with nature. It is a place which honors creation for its own sake and for what it adds to the understanding of the race. It is a place where men are more concerned with the quality of their goals than the quantity of their goods. But most of all, the Great Society is not a safe harbor, a resting place, a final objective, a finished work. It is a challenge constantly renewed, beckoning us toward a destiny where the meaning of our lives matches the marvelous products of our labor.

So I want to talk to you today about three places where we begin to build the Great Society—in our cities, in our countryside, and in our classrooms. Many of you will live to see the day, perhaps fifty years from now, when there will be four hundred million Americans; four-fifths of them in urban areas. In the remainder of this century urban population will double, city land will double, and we will have to build homes, highways and facilities equal to all those built since this country was first settled. So in the next forty years we must rebuild the entire urban United States.

Aristotle said, "Men come together in cities in order to live, but they remain together in order to live the good life."

It is harder and harder to live the good life in American cities today. The catalogue of ills is long: There is the decay of the centers and the despoiling of the suburbs. There is not enough housing for our people or transportation for our traffic. Open land is vanishing and old landmarks are violated. Worst of all, expansion is eroding the precious and time-honored values of community with neighbors and communion with nature. The loss of these values breeds loneliness and boredom and indifference. Our society will never be great until our cities are great. Today the frontier of imagination and innovation is inside those cities, and not beyond their borders. New experiments are already going on. It will be the task of your generation to make the American city a place where future generations will come, not only to live but to live the good life.

I understand that if I stay here tonight I would see that Michigan students are really doing their best to live the good life.

This is the place where the Peace Corps was started. It is inspiring to see how all of you, while you are in this country, are trying so hard to live at the level of the people.

A second place where we begin to build the Great Society is in our countryside. We have always prided ourselves on being not only America the strong and America the free, but America the beautiful. Today that beauty is in danger. The water we drink, the food we eat, the very air that we breathe, are threatened with pollution. Our parks are overcrowded. Our seashores overburdened. Green fields and dense forests are disappearing.

A few years ago we were greatly concerned about the Ugly American. Today we must act to prevent an Ugly America.

For once the battle is lost, once our natural splendor is destroyed, it can never be recaptured. And once man can no longer walk with beauty or wonder at nature, his spirit will wither and his sustenance be wasted.

A third place to build the Great Society is in the classrooms of America. There your children's lives will be shaped. Our society will not be great until every young mind is set free to scan the farthest reaches of thought and imagination. We are still far from that goal. Today, eight million adult Americans, more than the entire population of Michigan, have not finished five years of school. Nearly twenty million have not finished eight years of school. Nearly fifty-four million, more than one-quarter of all America, have not even finished high school.

Each year more than a hundred thousand high school graduates, with proved ability, do not enter college because they cannot afford it. And if we cannot educate today's youth, what will we do in 1970 when elementary school enrollment will be five million greater than 1960? And high school enrollment will rise by five million. College enrollment will increase by more than three million. In many places, classrooms are overcrowded and curricula are outdated. Most of our qualified teachers are underpaid, and many of our paid teachers are unqualified. So we must give every child a place to sit and a teacher to learn from.

Poverty must not be a bar to learning, and learning must offer an escape from poverty.

But more classrooms and more teachers are not enough. We must seek an educational system which grows in excellence as it grows in size. This means better training for our teachers. It means preparing youth to enjoy their hours of leisure as well as their hours of labor. It means exploring new techniques of teaching, to find new ways to stimulate the love of learning and the capacity for creation.

These are three of the central issues of the Great Society. While our government has many programs directed at those issues, I do not pretend that we have the full answer to those problems. But I do promise this: We are going to assemble the best thought and the broadest knowledge from all over the world to find those answers for America. I intend to establish working groups to prepare a series of White House conferences and meetings on the cities, on natural beauty, on the quality of education, and on other emerging challenges. And from these meetings and from this inspiration and from these studies we will begin to set our course toward the Great Society.

The solution to these problems does not rest on a massive program in Washington, nor can it rely solely on the strained resources of local authority. They require us to create new concepts of cooperation, a creative federalism, between the national Capitol and the leaders of local communities.

Woodrow Wilson once wrote: "Every man sent out from his university should be a man of his nation as well as a man of his time."

Within your lifetime powerful forces, already loosened, will take us toward a way of life beyond the realm of our experience, almost beyond the bounds of our imagination. For better or for worse, your generation has been appointed by history to deal with those problems and to lead America toward a new age. You have the chance never before afforded to any people in any age. You can help build a society where the demands of morality, and the needs of the spirit, can be realized in the life of the nation. So will you join in the battle to give every citizen the full equality which God enjoins and the law requires, whatever his belief, or race, or the color of his skin? Will you join in the battle to give every citizen an escape from the crushing weight of poverty? Will you join in the battle to make it possible for all nations to live in enduring peace as neighbors and not as mortal enemies? Will you join in the battle to build the Great Society, to prove that our material progress is only the foundation on which we will build a richer life of mind and spirit?

There are those timid souls who say this battle cannot be won, that we are condemned to a soulless wealth. I do not agree. We have the power to shape the civilization that we want. But we need your will, your labor, your hearts, if we are to build that kind of society.

Those who came to this land sought to build more than just a new country. They sought a free world.

So I have come here today to your campus to say that you can make their vision our reality. Let us from this moment begin our work so that in the future men will look back and say: It was then, after a long and weary way, that man turned the exploits of his genius to the full enrichment of his life.

Thank you. Goodbye.

——— ★ ———

PART FIVE

Patriotism and Praise

FROM ITS EARLIEST YEARS, the government of the new republic was different from that of any European country and its people were imbued with a new spirit. J. Hector St. John de Crèvecoeur and Alexis de Tocqueville were Frenchmen who lived for a while in the United States and wrote books recording their observations. They both described Americans as people of intense energy, self-reliance, and restlessness—hard-working and optimistic, fueled by a democratic attitude free of traditional social or class constraints.

This pride in democratic principles resulted in a literature steeped in patriotic expression, its poetry praising not a king or a religion but a flag and a concept. Walt Whitman wrote "For You O Democracy," Henry Ward Beecher spoke on the meaning of the flag, and Francis Scott Key and Joseph Rodman Drake, among many others, sang its praises in verse.

Inspired by the French government's gift to the United States of the Statue of Liberty, Emma Lazarus lauded the welcoming arms of the American nation in "The New Colossus." Theodore Roosevelt, as governor of New York, proudly explained the complexities and character of the presidency for the readers of the *Youth's Companion*. And as the greatest war in history raged across the Atlantic, Franklin Delano Roosevelt, in his third inaugural address, eloquently spoke about the unending vitality of American democracy.

What Is an American?

I wish I could be acquainted with the feelings and thoughts which must agitate the heart and present themselves to the mind of an enlightened Englishman, when he first lands on this continent. He must greatly rejoice that he lived at a time to see this fair country discovered and settled. He must necessarily feel a share of national pride when he views the chain of settlements which embellish these extended shores. When he says to himself, This is the work of my countrymen, who, when convulsed by factions, afflicted by a variety of miseries and wants, restless and impatient, took refuge here. They brought along with them their national genius, to which they principally owe what liberty they enjoy and what substance they possess. Here he sees the industry of his native country displayed in a new manner, and traces, in their works, the embryos of all the arts, sciences, and ingenuity, which flourish in Europe. Here he beholds fair cities, substantial villages, extensive fields, an immense country filled with decent houses, good roads, orchards, meadows, and bridges, where, a hundred years ago, all was wild, wooded, and uncultivated! What a train of pleasing ideas this fair spectacle must suggest! It is a prospect which must inspire a good citizen with the most heartfelt pleasure!

The difficulty consists in the manner of viewing so extensive a scene. He is arrived on a new continent: a modern society offers itself to his contemplation, different from what he had hitherto seen. It is not composed, as in Europe, of great lords who possess everything, and of a herd of people who have nothing. Here are no aristocratical families, no courts, no kings, no bishops, no ecclesiastical dominion, no invisible power giving to a few a very visible one, no great manufactures employing thousands, no great refinements of luxury. The rich and the poor are not so far removed from each other as they are in Europe. Some few towns excepted, we are all tillers of the earth, from Nova Scotia to West Florida. We are a people of cultivators, scattered over an immense territory, communicating with each other by means of good roads and navigable rivers, united by the silken bands of mild government, all respecting the laws, without dreading their power, because they are equitable. We are all animated with the spirit of an industry which is unfettered and unrestrained, because each person works for himself. If he travels through our rural districts, he views not the hostile castle and the haughty mansion contrasted with the clay-built hut and the miserable cabin, where cattle and men help to keep each other warm, and dwell in meanness, smoke, and indigence. A pleasing uniformity of decent competence appears throughout our habitations. The meanest of our log-houses is a dry and comfortable habitation. Lawyer or merchant are the fairest titles our towns afford: that of a farmer is the only appellation of the rural inhabitants of our country. It must take some time ere he can reconcile himself to our dictionary, which is but short in words of dignity and names of honor. There, on a Sunday, he sees a congregation of respectable farmers and their wives, all clad in neat homespun, well mounted, or riding in their own humble wagons. There is not among them an esquire, saving the unlettered magistrate. There he sees a parson as simple as his flock, a farmer who does not riot on the labor of others. We have no princes, for whom we toil, starve, and bleed. We are the most perfect society now existing in the world. Here man is free as he ought to be; nor is this pleasing equality so transitory as many others are. Many ages will not see the shores of our great lakes replenished with inland nations, nor the unknown bounds of North America entirely peopled. Who can tell how far it extends? Who can tell the millions of men whom it will feed and contain? For no European foot has, as yet, traveled half the extent of this mighty continent.

The next wish of this traveler will be, to know whence came all these people? They are a mixture of English, Scotch, Irish, French, Dutch, Germans, and Swedes. From this promiscuous breed, that race, now called Americans, have arisen. The eastern provinces must indeed be excepted, as being the unmixed descendants of Englishmen. I have heard many wish that they had been more intermixed also: for my part, I am no wisher, and think it much better as it has happened. They exhibit a most conspicuous figure in this great and variegated picture. They too enter for a great share in the pleasing perspective displayed in these thirteen provinces. I know it is fashionable to reflect on them, but I respect them for what they have done; for the activity and wisdom with which they have settled their territory; for the decency of their manners; for their early love of letters; their ancient college, the first in this hemisphere; for their industry, which to me, who am but a farmer, is the criterion of everything. There never was a people, situated as they are, who, with so ungrateful a soil, have done more in so short a time. . . .

Urged by a variety of motives here they came. Everything has tended to regenerate them. New laws, a new mode of living, a new social system. Here they are become men. In Europe they were as so many useless plants, wanting vegetative mould and refreshing showers. They withered, and were mowed down by want, hunger, and war; but now, by the power of transplantation, like all other plants, they have taken root and flourished! Formerly they were not numbered in any civil lists of their country, except in those of the poor; here they rank as citizens. By what invisible power has this surprising metamorphosis been performed? By that of the laws and that of their industry. The laws, the indulgent laws, protect them as they arrive, stamping on them the symbol of adoption; they receive ample rewards for their labors; these accumulated rewards procure them lands; those lands confer on them the title of freemen, and to that title every benefit is affixed which men can possibly require. This is the great operation daily performed by our laws. Whence proceed these laws? From our government. Whence that government? It is derived from the original genius and strong desire of the people ratified and confirmed by the crown. This is the great chain which links us all; this is the picture which every province exhibits, Nova Scotia excepted. . . .

What then is the American, this new man? He is neither a European, nor the descendant of a European; hence that strange mixture of blood, which you will find in no other country. I could point out to you a family, whose grandfather was an Englishman, whose wife was Dutch, whose son married a French woman, and whose present four sons have now four wives of different nations. He is an American, who, leaving behind him all his ancient prejudices and manners, receives new ones from the new mode of life he has embraced, the new government he obeys, and the new rank he holds. He becomes an American by being received in the broad lap of our great alma mater. Here individuals of all nations are melted into a new race of men, whose labors and posterity will one day cause great changes in the world. Americans are the western pilgrims, who are carrying along with them the great mass of arts, sciences, vigor, and industry, which began long since in the East. They will finish the great circle. The Americans were once scattered all over Europe. Here they are incorporated into one of the finest systems of population which has ever appeared, and which will hereafter become distinct by the power of the different climates they inhabit. The American ought therefore to love this country much better than that in which either he or his forefathers were born. Here the rewards of his industry follow, with equal steps, the progress of his labor. His labor is founded on the basis of nature, self-interest: can it want a stronger allurement? Wives and children, who before in vain demanded of him a morsel of bread, now, fat and frolicsome, gladly help their father to clear those fields whence exuberant crops are to raise, to feed and to clothe them all, without any part being claimed, either by a despotic prince, a rich abbot, or a mighty lord. Here religion demands but little of him; a small voluntary salary to the minister, and gratitude to God: can he refuse these?

The American is a new man, who acts on new principles; he must therefore entertain new ideas and form new opinions. From involuntary idleness, servile dependence, penury, and useless labor, he has passed to toils of a very different nature, rewarded by ample subsistence. This is an American.

J. HECTOR ST. JOHN DE CRÈVECOEUR,
from *Letters from an American Farmer,* 1782

HAIL! COLUMBIA

Hail! Columbia happy land,
Hail! ye heroes heav'n born band
   Who fought and bled in freedom's cause,
   Who fought and bled in freedom's cause
And when the storm of war was gone
Enjoy'd the peace your valor won.
   Let independence be our boast,
   Ever mindful what it cost;
   Ever grateful for the prize,
   Let its altar reach the skies.

Firm united let us be
Rallying round our liberty
As a band of brothers join'd,
Peace and safety we shall find.

Immortal patriots rise once more,
Defend your rights—defend your shore.
   Let no rude foe with impious hand,
   Let no rude foe with impious hand

Invade the shrine where sacred lies
Of toil and blood the well-earned prize
    While off'ring peace, sincere and just;
    In heav'n we place a manly trust
    That truth and justice may prevail
    And ev'ry scheme of bondage fail.

Sound sound the trump of fame,
Let Washington's great name
    Ring thro' the world with loud applause,
    Ring thro' the world with loud applause,
Let ev'ry clime to freedom dear
Listen with a joyful ear—
    With equal skill with godlike pow'r
    He governs in the fearful hour
    Of horrid war or guides with ease
    The happier times of honest peace.

Behold the chief who now commands,
Once more to serve his country stands
    The rock on which the storm will beat,
    The rock on which the storm will beat.
But arm'd in virtue firm and true
His hopes are fixed on heav'n and you—
    When hope was sinking in dismay,
    When glooms obscur'd Columbia's day,
    His steady mind from changes free
    Resolv'd on death or liberty.

JOSEPH HOPKINSON

AMERICAN COLLEGES

To nurse the arts and fashion freedom's lore
Young schools of science rise along the shore;
Great without pomp their modest walls expand,
Harvard and Yale and Princeton grace the land,
Penn's student halls his youths with gladness greet,
On James's bank Virginian Muses meet,
Manhattan's mart collegiate domes command,
Bosom'd in groves, see growing Dartmouth stand;
Bright o'er its realm reflecting solar fires,
On yon tall hill Rhode Island's seat expires.
Thousands of humbler name around them rise,
Where homebred freemen seize the solid prize;
Fixt in small spheres, with safer beams to shine,
They reach the useful and refuse the fine,
Found, on its proper base, the social plan,
The broad plain truths, the common sense of man,
His obvious wants, his mutual aids discern,
His rights familiarize, his duties learn,
Feel moral fitness all its force dilate,
Embrace the village and comprise the state.
Each rustic here who turns the furrow'd soil,
The maid, the youth that ply mechanic toil,
In equal rights, in useful arts inured,
Know their just claims, and see their claims secured;
They watch their delegates, each law revise,
Its faults designate and its merits prize,
Obey, but scrutinize; and let the test
Of sage experience prove and fix the best.

JOEL BARLOW,
from *The Columbiad,* 1807

AMERICAN SCIENCE

And lo, my son, that other sapient band,
The torch of science flaming in their hand!
Through nature's range their searching souls aspire,
Or wake to life the canvas and the lyre.
Fixt in sublimest thought, behold them rise
World after world unfolding to their eyes,
Lead, light, allure them through the total plan,
And give new guidance to the paths of man.
Yon meteor-mantled hill see Franklin tread,
Heaven's awful thunders rolling o'er his head;
Convolving clouds the billowy skies deform,
And forky flames emblaze the blackening storm.
See the descending streams around him burn,
Glance on his rod and with his finger turn;
He bids conflicting fulminants expire
The guided blast, and holds the imprison'd fire.
No more, when doubling storms the vault o'erspread,
The livid glare shall strike thy race with dread,
Nor towers nor temples, shuddering with the sound,
Sink in the flames and shake the sheeted ground.
His well-tried wires, that every tempest wait,
Shall teach mankind to ward the bolts of fate,
With pointed steel o'ertop the trembling spire,
And lead from untouch'd walls the harmless fire;
Fill'd with his fame while distant climes rejoice,
Wherever lightning shines or thunder rears its voice.

JOEL BARLOW,
from *The Columbiad*, 1807

AMERICAN POETRY

To equal fame ascends thy tuneful throng,
The boast of genius and the pride of song;
Caught from the cast of every age and clime,
Their lays shall triumph o'er the lapse of time.
With lynx-eyed glance through nature far to pierce,
With all the powers and every charm of verse,
Each science opening in his ample mind,
His fancy glowing and his taste refined,
See Trumbull lead the train. His skillful hand
Hurls the keen darts of satire round the land.
Pride, knavery, dullness feel his mortal stings,
And listening virtue triumphs while he sings;
Britain's foil'd sons, victorious now no more,
In guilt retiring from the wasted shore,
Strive their curst cruelties to hide in vain;
The world resounds them in his deathless strain.
On wings of faith to elevate the soul
Beyond the bourn of earth's benighted pole,
For Dwight's high harp the epic Muse sublime
Hails her new empire in the western clime.
Tuned from the tones by seers seraphic sung,
Heaven in his eye and rapture on his tongue,
His voice revives old Canaan's promised land,
The long-fought fields of Jacob's chosen band.
In Hanniel's fate, proud faction finds its doom,
Ai's midnight flames light nations to their tomb,
In visions bright supernal joys are given,
And all the dark futurities of heaven.

JOEL BARLOW,
from *The Columbiad,* 1807

THE STAR-SPANGLED BANNER

O! say, can you see, by the dawn's early light,
    What so proudly we hailed at the twilight's last
        gleaming:
Whose broad stripes and bright stars, through the
        perilous fight,
    O'er the ramparts we watched were so gallantly
        streaming,
And the rocket's red glare, the bombs bursting in air,
Gave proof through the night that our flag was still
        there;

    O! say, does the star-spangled banner still wave
    O'er the land of the free and the home of the brave?

On the shore, dimly seen through the mist of the deep,
    Where the foe's haughty host in dread silence reposes,
What is that which the breeze, o'er the towering steep,
    As it fitfully blows, half conceals, half discloses?
Now it catches the gleam of the morning's first beam—
In full glory reflected, now shines on the stream;

    'Tis the star-spangled banner, O! long may it wave
    O'er the land of the free and the home of the brave.

And where is the band who so vauntingly swore
    That the havoc of war and the battle's confusion
A home and a country would leave us no more?
    Their blood has washed out their foul footsteps' pollution.
No refuge could save the hireling and slave
From the terror of flight or the gloom of the grave!

    And the star-spangled banner in triumph doth wave
    O'er the land of the free and the home of the brave.

O! thus be it ever when freemen shall stand
  Between their loved homes and the foe's desolation;
Bless'd with victory and peace, may our heaven-rescued land
  Praise the Power that hath made and preserved us a
    nation.
Then conquer we must, for our cause it is just—
And this be our motto—"In God is our trust!"

  And the star-spangled banner in triumph shall wave
  O'er the land of the free and the home of the brave.

FRANCIS SCOTT KEY

THE AMERICAN FLAG

When Freedom, from her mountain height,
  Unfurled her standard to the air,
She tore the azure robe of night,
  And set the stars of glory there!
She mingled with its gorgeous dyes
The milky baldric of the skies,
And striped its pure celestial white
With streakings of the morning light,
Then, from his mansion in the sun,
She called her eagle-bearer down,
And gave into his mighty hand
The symbol of her chosen land!

Majestic monarch of the cloud!
  Who rear'st aloft thy regal form,
To hear the tempest-tramping loud,
And see the lightning-lances driven,
  When stride the warriors of the storm,

And rolls the thunder-drum of heaven!
Child of the sun! to thee 'tis given
  To guard the banner of the free,
To hover in the sulphur smoke,
To ward away the battle stroke,
And bid its blendings shine afar,
Like rainbows on the cloud of war,
  The harbingers of victory!

Flag of the brave! thy folds shall fly,
The sign of hope and triumph high!
When speaks the signal-trumpet tone,
And the long line comes gleaming on,
Ere yet the life-blood, warm and wet,
Has dimmed the glist'ning bayonet,
Each soldier's eye shall brightly turn
To where thy meteor-glories burn,
And, as his springing steps advance,
Catch war and vengeance from the glance!

And when the cannon-mouthings loud
Heave in wild wreaths the battle-shroud,
And gory sabres rise and fall,
Like shoots of flame on midnight's pall!
  Then shall thy meteor-glances glow,
And cowering foes shall shrink beneath,
  Each gallant arm that strikes below,
The lovely messenger of death.

Flag of the seas! on ocean's wave
Thy stars shall glitter o'er the brave;
When Death, careering on the gale,
Sweeps darkly round the bellied sail,
And frighted waves rush wildly back
Before the broadside's reeling rack,

The dying wanderer of the sea
Shall look, at once, to heaven and thee,
And smile, to see thy splendors fly,
In triumph, o'er his closing eye.

Flag of the free heart's hope and home,
    By angel hands to valor given!
Thy stars have lit the welkin dome,
    And all thy hues were born in heaven!
Forever float that standard sheet!
    Where breathes the foe but falls before us?
With freedom's soil beneath our feet,
    And freedom's banner streaming o'er us!

JOSEPH RODMAN DRAKE

America

My country 'tis of thee
Sweet land of liberty:
　Of thee I sing.
Land where my fathers died
Land of the pilgrims' pride
From every mountainside
　Let freedom ring.

My native country—thee
Land of the noble free
　Thy name I love;
I love thy rocks and rills
Thy woods and templed hills
My heart with rapture thrills
　Like that above.

Let music swell the breeze
And ring from all the trees
　Sweet freedom's song
Let all that breathe partake
Let mortal tongues awake
Let rocks their silence break
　The sound prolong.

Our fathers' God to thee
Author of liberty
　To thee we sing
Long may our land be bright
With freedom's holy light
Protect us by thy might
　Great God, our King.

SAMUEL SMITH

From Colonel William Barret Travis to the People of Texas: At the Alamo

Commandancy of the Alamo
Fby. 24th 1836

To the People of Texas & all Americans *in the world*—

Fellow Citizens & Compatriots: I am besieged, by a thousand or more of the Mexicans under Santa Anna—I have sustained a continual Bombardment & cannonade for 24 hours & have not lost a man—The enemy has demanded a surrender at discretion, otherwise the garrison are to be put to the *sword,* if the fort is taken—I have answered the demand with a cannon shot, & our flag still waves proudly from the walls—*I shall never surrender or retreat. Then,* I call on you in the name of Liberty, of patriotism & everything dear to the American character, to come to our aid, with all dispatch—The enemy is receiving reinforcements daily & will no doubt increase to three or four thousand in four or five days. If this call is neglected, I am determined to sustain myself as long as possible & die like a soldier who never forgets what is due to his own honor & that of his country—

VICTORY OR DEATH

WILLIAM BARRET TRAVIS
Lt. Col. Comdt.

P.S. The Lord is on our side—When the enemy appeared in sight we had not three bushels of corn—We have since found in deserted houses 80 or 90 bushels & got into the walls 20 or 30 head of Beeves—

TRAVIS

239

The Defense of the Alamo

March 6, 1836

Santa Ana came storming, as a storm might come;
   There was rumble of cannon; there was rattle of blade;
There was cavalry, infantry, bugle, and drum—
   Full seven thousand in pomp and parade.
The chivalry, flower of Mexico;
And a gaunt two hundred in the Alamo!

And thirty lay sick, and some were shot through;
   For the siege had been bitter, and bloody, and long.
"Surrender, or die!"—"Men, what will *you* do?"
   And Travis, great Travis, drew sword, quick and strong;
Drew a line at his feet. . . . "Will you come? Will you go?
I die with my wounded, in the Alamo."

Then Bowie gasped, "Lead me over that line!"
   Then Crockett, one hand to the sick, one hand to his gun,
Crossed with him; then never a word or a sign
   Till all, sick or well, all, all save but one,
One man. Then a woman stepped, praying, and slow
Across; to die at her post in the Alamo.

Then that one coward fled, in the night, in that night
   When all men silently prayed and thought
Of home; of tomorrow; of God and the right,
   Till dawn; and with dawn came Travis's cannon-shot,
In answer to insolent Mexico,
From the old bell-tower of the Alamo.

Then came Santa Ana; a crescent of flame!
   Then the red escalade; then the fight hand to hand;
Such an unequal fight as never had name

Since the Persian hordes butchered that doomed Spartan
   band.
All day—all day and all night; and the morning? so slow,
Through the battle smoke mantling the Alamo.

Now silence! Such silence! Two thousand lay dead
   In a crescent outside! And within? Not a breath
Save the gasp of a woman, with gory gashed head,
   All alone, all alone there, waiting for death;
And she but a nurse. Yet when shall we know
Another like this of the Alamo?

Shout, "Victory, victory, victory ho!"
   I say 'tis not always to the hosts that win!
I say that the victory, high or low,
   Is given the hero who grapples with sin,
Or legion or single; just asking to know
When duty fronts death in his Alamo.

                                        Joaquin Miller

THE AMERICAN CHARACTER

PUBLIC ASSOCIATIONS IN CIVIL LIFE

The political associations that exist in the United States are only a single feature in the midst of the immense assemblage of associations in that country. Americans of all ages, all conditions, and all dispositions constantly form associations. They have not only commercial and manufacturing companies, in which all take part, but associations of a thousand other kinds, religious, moral, serious, futile, general or restricted, enormous or diminutive. The Americans make associations to give entertainments, to found seminaries, to build inns, to construct churches, to diffuse books, to send missionaries to the antipodes; in this manner they found hospitals, prisons, and schools. If it is proposed to inculcate some truth or to foster some feeling by the encouragement of a great example, they form a society. Wherever at the head of some new undertaking you see the government in France, or a man of rank in England, in the United States you will be sure to find an association.

I met with several kinds of associations in America of which I confess I had no previous notion; and I have often admired the extreme skill with which the inhabitants of the United States succeed in proposing a common object for the exertions of a great many men and in inducing them voluntarily to pursue it.

I have since traveled over England, from which the Americans have taken some of their laws and many of their customs; and it seemed to me that the principle of association was by no means so constantly or adroitly used in that country. The English often perform great things singly, whereas the Americans form associations for the smallest undertakings. It is evident that the former people consider association as a powerful means of action, but the latter seem to regard it as the only means they have of acting.

Thus the most democratic country on the face of the earth is that in which men have, in our time, carried to the highest perfection the art of pursuing in common the object of their common desires and have applied this new science to the greatest number of purposes. Is this the result of accident, or is there in reality any necessary connection between the principle of association and that of equality? . . .

Among democratic nations . . . all the citizens are independent and feeble; they can do hardly anything by themselves, and none of them can oblige his fellow men to lend him their assistance. They all, therefore, become powerless if they do not learn voluntarily to help one another. If men living in democratic countries had no right and no inclination to associate for political purposes, their independence would be in great jeopardy, but they might long preserve their wealth and their cultivation: whereas if they never acquired the habit of forming associations in ordinary life, civilization itself would be endangered. . . .

Unhappily, the same social condition that renders associations so necessary to democratic nations renders their formation more difficult among those nations than among all others. When several members of an aristocracy agree to combine, they easily succeed in doing so; as each of them brings great strength to the partnership, the number of its members may be very limited; and when the members of an association are limited in number, they may easily become mutually acquainted, understand each other, and establish fixed regulations. The same opportunities do not occur among democratic nations, where the associated members must always be very numerous for their association to have any power. . . .

A government might perform the part of some of the largest American companies, and several states, members of the Union, have already attempted it; but what political power could ever carry on the vast multitude of lesser undertakings which the American citizens perform every day, with the assistance of the principle of association? It is easy to foresee that the time is drawing near when man will be less and less able to produce, by himself alone, the commonest necessaries of life. The task of the governing power will therefore perpetually increase, and its very efforts will extend it every day. The more it stands in the place of associations, the more will individuals, losing the notion of combining together, require its assistance: these are causes and effects that unceasingly create each other. . . .

As soon as several of the inhabitants of the United States have taken up an opinion or a feeling which they wish to promote in the world, they look out for mutual assistance; and as soon as they have found one another out, they combine. From that moment they are no longer isolated men, but a power seen from afar, whose actions serve for an example and whose language is listened to. The first time I heard in the United States that a hundred thousand men had bound themselves publicly to abstain from spirituous liquors, it appeared to me more like a joke than a serious engagement, and I did not at once perceive why these temperate citizens could not content themselves with drinking water by their own firesides. I at last understood that these hundred thousand Americans, alarmed by the progress of drunkenness around them, had made up their minds to patronize temperance. They acted in just the same way as a man of high rank who should dress very plainly in order to inspire the humbler orders with a contempt of luxury. It is probable that if these hundred thousand men had lived in France, each of them would singly have memorialized the government to watch the public houses all over the kingdom.

Nothing, in my opinion, is more deserving of our attention than the intellectual and moral associations of America. The political and industrial associations of that country strike us forcibly; but the others elude our observation, or if we discover them, we understand them imperfectly because we have hardly ever seen anything of the kind. It must be acknowledged, however, that they are as necessary to the American people as the former, and perhaps more so. In democratic countries the science of association is the mother of science; the progress of all the rest depends upon the progress it has made.

Among the laws that rule human societies there is one which seems to be more precise and clear than all others. If men are to remain civilized or to become so, the art of associating together must grow and improve in the same ratio in which the equality of conditions is increased.

SELF-INTEREST RIGHTLY UNDERSTOOD

In the United States hardly anybody talks of the beauty of virtue, but they maintain that virtue is useful and prove it every day. The American moralists do not profess that men ought to sacrifice themselves for their fellow creatures because it is noble to make such sacrifices, but they boldly aver that such sacrifices are as necessary to him who imposes them upon himself as to him for whose sake they are made.

They have found out that, in their country and their age, man is brought home to himself by an irresistible force; and, losing all hope of stopping that force, they turn all their thoughts to the direction of it. They therefore do not deny that every man may follow his own interest, but they endeavor to prove that it is the interest of every man to be virtuous. I shall not here enter into the reasons they allege, which would divert me from my subject; suffice it to say that they have convinced their fellow countrymen.

Montaigne said long ago: "Were I not to follow the straight road for its straightness, I should follow it for having found by experience that in the end it is commonly the happiest and most useful track." The doctrine of interest rightly understood is not then new, but among the Americans of our time it finds universal acceptance; it has become popular there; you may trace it at the bottom of all their actions, you will remark it in all they say. It is as often asserted by the poor man as by the rich. In Europe the principle of interest is much grosser than it is in America, but it is also less common and especially it is less avowed; among us, men still constantly feign great abnegation which they no longer feel.

The Americans, on the other hand, are fond of explaining almost all the actions of their lives by the principle of self-interest rightly understood; they show with complacency how an enlightened regard for themselves constantly prompts them to assist one another and inclines them willingly to sacrifice a portion of their time and property to the welfare of the state. In this respect I think they frequently fail to do themselves justice; for in the United States as well as elsewhere people are sometimes seen to give way to those disinterested and spontaneous impulses that are natural to man; but the Americans seldom admit that they yield to emotions of this kind; they are more anxious to do honor to their philosophy than to themselves. . . .

The principle of self-interest rightly understood produces no great acts of self-sacrifice, but it suggests daily small acts of self-denial. By itself it cannot suffice to make a man virtuous; but it disciplines a number of persons in habits of regularity, temperance, moderation, foresight, self-command; and if it does not lead men straight to virtue by the will, it gradually draws them in that direction by their habits. If the principle of interest rightly understood were to sway the whole moral world, extraordinary virtues would doubtless be more rare; but I think that gross depravity would then also be less common. The principle of interest rightly understood perhaps prevents men from rising far above the level of mankind, but a great number of other men, who were falling far below it, are caught and restrained by it. Observe some few individuals, they are lowered by it; survey mankind, they are raised.

I am not afraid to say that the principle of self-interest rightly understood appears to me the best suited of all philosophical theories to the wants of the men of our time, and that I regard it as their chief remaining security against themselves. Toward it, therefore, the minds of the moralists of our age should turn; even should they judge it to be incomplete, it must nevertheless be adopted as necessary.

I do not think, on the whole, that there is more selfishness among us than in America; the only difference is that there it is enlightened, here it is not. Each American knows when to sacrifice some of his private interests to save the rest; we want to save everything, and often we lose it all. Everybody I see about me seems bent on teaching his contemporaries, by precept and example, that what is useful is never wrong. Will nobody undertake to make them understand how what is right may be useful?

No power on earth can prevent the increasing equality of conditions from inclining the human mind to seek out what is useful or from leading every member of the community to be wrapped up in himself. It must therefore be expected that personal interest will become more than ever the principal if not the sole spring of men's actions; but it remains to be seen how each man will understand his personal interest. If the members of a community, as they become more equal, become more ignorant and coarse, it is difficult to foresee to what pitch of stupid excesses their selfishness may lead them; and no one can foretell into what disgrace and wretchedness they would plunge themselves lest they should have to sacrifice something of their own well-being to the prosperity of their fellow creatures.

I do not think that the system of self-interest as it is professed in America is in all its parts self-evident, but it contains a great number of truths so evident that men, if they are only educated, cannot fail to see them. Educate, then, at any rate, for the age of implicit self-sacrifice and instinctive virtues is already flitting far away from us, and the time is fast approaching when freedom, public peace, and social order itself will not be able to exist without education.

ALL HONEST CALLINGS ARE CONSIDERED HONORABLE

Among a democratic people, where there is no hereditary wealth, every man works to earn a living, or has worked, or is born of parents who have worked. The notion of labor is therefore presented to the mind, on every side, as the necessary, natural, and honest condition of human existence. Not only is labor not dishonorable among such a people, but it is held in honor; the prejudice is not against it, but in its favor. In the United States a wealthy man thinks that he owes it to public opinion to devote his leisure to some kind of industrial or commercial pursuit or to public business. He would think himself in bad repute if he employed his life solely in living. It is for the purpose of escaping this obligation to work that so many rich Americans come to Europe, where they find some scattered remains of aristocratic society, among whom idleness is still held in honor.

Equality of conditions not only ennobles the notion of labor, but raises the notion of labor as a source of profit.

In aristocracies it is not exactly labor that is despised, but labor with a view to profit. Labor is honorable in itself when it is undertaken at the bidding of ambition or virtue. Yet in aristocratic society it constantly happens that he who works for honor is not insensible to the attractions of profit. But these two desires intermingle only in the depths of his soul; he carefully hides from every eye the point at which they join; he would gladly conceal it from himself. In aristocratic countries there are few public officers who do not affect to serve their country without interested motives. Their salary is an incident of which they think but little and of which they always affect not to think at all. Thus the notion of profit is kept distinct from that of labor; however they may be united in point of fact, they are not thought of together.

In democratic communities these two notions are, on the contrary, always palpably united. As the desire of well-being is universal, as fortunes are slender or fluctuating, as everyone wants either to increase his own resources or to provide fresh ones for his progeny, men clearly see that it is profit that, if not wholly, at least partially leads them to work. Even those who are principally actuated by the love of fame are necessarily made familiar with the thought that they are not exclusively actuated by that motive; and they discover that the desire of getting a living is mingled in their minds with the desire of making life illustrious.

As soon as, on the one hand, labor is held by the whole community to be an honorable necessity of man's condition, and, on the other, as soon as labor is always ostensibly performed, wholly or in part, for the purpose of earning remuneration, the immense interval that separated different callings in aristocratic societies disappears. If all are not alike, all at least have one feature in common. No profession exists in which men do not work for money; and the remuneration that is common to them all gives them all an air of resemblance.

This serves to explain the opinions that the Americans entertain with respect to different callings. In America no one is degraded because he works, for everyone about him works also; nor is anyone humiliated by the notion of receiving pay, for the president of the United States also works for pay. He is paid for commanding, other men for obeying orders. In the United States professions are more or less laborious, more or less profitable; but they are never either high or low: every honest calling is honorable.

THE GRAVITY OF THE AMERICANS

Men who live in democratic countries do not value the simple, turbulent, or coarse diversions in which the people in aristocratic communities indulge; such diversions are thought by them to be puerile or insipid. Nor have they a greater inclination for the intellectual and refined amusements of the aristocratic classes. They want something productive and substantial in their pleasures; they want to mix actual fruition with their joy.

In aristocratic communities the people readily give themselves up to bursts of tumultuous and boisterous gaiety, which shake off at once the recollection of their privations. The inhabitants of democracies are not fond of being thus violently broken in upon, and they never lose sight of themselves without regret. Instead of these frivolous delights they prefer those more serious and silent amusements which are like business and which do not drive business wholly out of their minds.

An American, instead of going in a leisure hour to dance merrily at some place of public resort, as the fellows of his class continue to do throughout the greater part of Europe, shuts himself up at home to drink. He thus enjoys two pleasures; he can go on thinking of his business and can get drunk decently by his own fireside.

I thought that the English constituted the most serious nation on the face of the earth, but I have since seen the Americans and have changed my opinion. I do not mean to say that temperament has not a great deal to do with the character of the inhabitants of the United States, but I think that their political institutions are a still more influential cause.

I believe the seriousness of the Americans arises partly from their pride. In democratic countries even poor men entertain a lofty notion of their personal importance; they look upon themselves with complacency and are apt to suppose that others are looking at them too. With this disposition, they watch their language and their actions with care and do not lay themselves open so as to betray their deficiencies; to preserve their dignity, they think it necessary to retain their gravity.

But I detect another more deep-seated and powerful cause which instinctively produces among the Americans this astonishing gravity. Under a despotism communities give way at times to bursts of vehement joy, but they are generally gloomy and moody because they are afraid. Under absolute monarchies tempered by the customs and manners of the country, their spirits are often cheerful and even, because, as they have some freedom and a good deal of security, they are exempted from the most important cares of life; but all free nations are serious because their minds are habitually absorbed by the contemplation of some dangerous or difficult purpose. This is more especially the case among those free nations which form democratic communities. Then there is, in all classes, a large number of men constantly occupied with the serious affairs of the government;

and those whose thoughts are not engaged in the matters of the commonwealth are wholly engrossed by the acquisition of a private fortune. Among such a people a serious demeanor ceases to be peculiar to certain men and becomes a habit of the nation.

ALEXIS DE TOCQUEVILLE,
from *Democracy in America*, 1840

ODE

Sung in the Town Hall, Concord, July 4, 1857

O tenderly the haughty day
   Fills his blue urn with fire;
One morn is in the mighty heaven,
   And one in our desire.

The cannon booms from town to town,
   Our pulses beat not less,
The joy-bells chime their tidings down,
   Which children's voices bless.

For He that flung the broad blue fold
   O'er-mantling land and sea,
One third part of the sky unrolled
   For the banner of the free.

The men are ripe of Saxon kind
   To build an equal state—
To take the statute from the mind
   And make of duty fate.

United States! the ages plead—
   Present and past in under-song—
Go put your creed into your deed,
   Nor speak with double tongue.

For sea and land don't understand
   Nor skies without a frown
See rights for which the one hand fights
   By the other cloven down.

Be just at home; then write your scroll
   Of honor o'er the sea,
And bid the broad Atlantic roll
   A ferry of the free.

And henceforth there shall be no chain,
   Save underneath the sea
The wires shall murmur through the main
   Sweet songs of liberty.

The conscious stars accord above,
   The waters wild below,
And under, through the cable wove,
   Her fiery errands go.

For He that worketh high and wise,
   Nor pauses in his plan,
Will take the sun out of the skies
   Ere freedom out of man.

RALPH WALDO EMERSON

I Hear America Singing

I hear America singing, the varied carols I hear,
Those of mechanics, each one singing his as it should be
    blithe and strong,
The carpenter singing his as he measures his plank or beam,
The mason singing his as he makes ready for work, or leaves
    off work,
The boatman singing what belongs to him in his boat, the
    deck-hand singing on the steamboat deck,
The shoemaker singing as he sits on his bench, the hatter
    singing as he stands,
The woodcutter's song, the ploughboy's on his way in the
    morning, or at noon intermission or at sundown,
The delicious singing of the mother, or of the young wife at
    work, or of the girl sewing or washing,
Each singing what belongs to him or her and to none else,
The day what belongs to the day—at night the party of
    young fellows, robust, friendly,
Singing with open mouths their strong melodious songs.

WALT WHITMAN

FOR YOU O DEMOCRACY

Come, I will make the continent indissoluble,
I will make the most splendid race the sun ever shone upon,
I will make divine magnetic lands,
    With the love of comrades,
      With the life-long love of comrades.

I will plant companionship thick as trees along the rivers of
    America, and along the shores of the great lakes, and all
    over
    the prairies,

I will make inseparable cities with their arms about each
    other's
    necks,
      By the love of comrades,
      By the manly love of comrades,

For you these from me, O Democracy, to serve you ma
    femme!
For you, for you I am trilling these songs.

WALT WHITMAN

The National Flag

From the earliest periods nations seem to have gone forth to war under some banner. Sometimes it has been merely the pennon of a leader, and was only a rallying signal. So, doubtless, began the habit of carrying banners, to direct men in the confusion of conflict, that the leader might gather his followers around him when he himself was liable to be lost out of their sight.

Later in the history of nations the banner acquired other uses and peculiar significance from the parties, the orders, the houses, or governments, that adopted it. At length, as consolidated governments drank up into themselves all these lesser independent authorities, banners became significant chiefly of national authority. And thus in our day every people has its peculiar flag. There is no civilized nation without its banner.

A thoughtful mind, when it sees a nation's flag, sees not the flag but the nation itself. And whatever may be its symbols, its insignia, he reads chiefly in the flag the government, the principles, the truths, the history that belong to the nation that sets it forth. When the French tricolor rolls out to the wind, we see France. When the new-found Italian flag is unfurled, we see resurrected Italy. . . . When the united crosses of St. Andrew and St. George, on a fiery ground, set forth the banner of Old England, we see not the cloth merely; there rises up before the mind the idea of that great monarchy.

This nation has a banner, too. . . . The American flag has been a symbol of liberty, and men rejoiced in it. Not another flag on the globe had such an errand, or went forth upon the sea carrying everywhere, the world around, such hope to the captive and such glorious tidings. The stars upon it were to the pining nations like the bright morning stars of God, and the stripes upon it were beams of morning light. As at early dawn the stars shine forth even while it grows light, and then as the sun advances that light breaks into banks and streaming lines of color, the glowing red and intense white striving together, and ribbing the horizon with bars effulgent, so, on the American flag, stars and beams of many-colored light shine out together. And wherever this flag comes, and men behold it, they see in its sacred emblazonry no ramping lion, and no fierce eagle; no embattled castles, or insignia of imperial authority; they see the symbols of light. It is the banner of dawn. It means liberty; and the galley-slave, the poor, oppressed conscript, the trodden-down creature of foreign despotism, sees in the American flag that very promise and prediction of God—"The people which sat in darkness saw a great light; and to them which sat in the region and shadow of death light is sprung up."

Is this a mere fancy? On the fourth of July 1776, the Declaration of American Independence was confirmed and promulgated. Already for more than a year the colonies had been at war with the mother country. But until this time there had been no American flag. The flag of the mother country covered us during all our colonial period; and each state that chose had a separate and significant state banner.

In 1777, within a few days of one year after the Declaration of Independence, and two years and more after the war began, upon the fourteenth of June, the Congress of the colonies, or the confederated states, assembled, and ordained this glorious national flag which now we hold and defend, and advanced it full high before God and all men as the flag of liberty. It was no holiday flag, gorgeously emblazoned for gaiety or vanity. It was a solemn national signal. When that banner first unrolled to the sun, it was the symbol of all those holy truths and purposes which brought together the colonial American Congress.

Consider the men who devised and set forth this banner. The Rutledges, the Pinckneys, the Jays, the Franklins, the Hamiltons, the Jeffersons, the Adamses—these men were all either officially connected with it or consulted concerning it. They were men that had taken their lives in their hands, and consecrated all their worldly possessions—for what? For the doctrines, and for the personal fact, of liberty—for the right of *all* men to liberty. They had just given forth to the world a declaration of facts and faiths out of which sprung the Constitution, and on which they now planted this new-devised flag of our Union.

If one, then, asks me the meaning of our flag, I say to him, It means just what Concord and Lexington meant, what Bunker Hill meant; it means the whole glorious Revolutionary War, which was, in short, the rising up of a valiant young people against an old tyranny, to establish the most momentous doctrine that the world had ever known, or has since known—the right of men to their own selves and to their liberties.

In solemn conclave our fathers had issued to the world that glorious manifesto, the Declaration of Independence. A little later, that the fundamental principles of liberty might have the best organization, they gave to this land our imperishable Constitution. Our flag means, then, all that our fathers meant in the Revolutionary War; all that the Declaration of Independence meant; it means all that the Constitution of our people, organizing for justice, for liberty, and for happiness, meant. Our flag carries American ideas, American history, and American feelings. Beginning with the colonies, and coming down to our time, in its sacred heraldry, in its glorious insignia, it has gathered and stored chiefly this supreme idea: *Divine right of liberty in man.* Every color means liberty; every thread means liberty; every form of star and beam or stripe of light means liberty; not lawlessness, not license; but organized, institutional liberty— liberty through law, and laws for liberty!

This American flag was the safeguard of liberty. Not an atom of crown was allowed to go into its insignia. Not a symbol of authority in the ruler was permitted to go into it. It was an ordinance of liberty by the people for the people. *That* it meant, *that* it means, and by the blessing of God, *that* it shall mean to the end of time!

> HENRY WARD BEECHER,
> from an address at Plymouth Congregational Church,
> Brooklyn, New York, 1861

HYMN FOR THE FOURTH OF JULY

Our fathers built the house of God;
Rough-hewn, with haste its slabs they laid,
The savage man in ambush trod,
And still they worshiped undismayed.

They wrought like stalwart men of war,
Who wrung the state from heathen hands;
Who bore their faith's high banner far,
And in its name possessed the lands.

The skill of strife to peaceful arts,
Their perils over, glad gave way;
The bond of freedom joined men's hearts
More near than meaner compact may.

We, followers of their task and toil,
Inherited their dangers too;
Drove bloody rapine from our soil,
Th' oppressor dared, the murderer slew.

Our heavy work, like theirs, at end;
Returning from the death-won field,
Brother with brother, friend with friend
Again the house of God we build.

Oh! may our ransomed freedom dwell
In truth's own citadel secure;
And blameless guardians foster well
The mystic flame that must endure.

The flame of holy human love,
That makes our liberties divine;
Let each strong arm its champion prove,
And each true heart its deathless shrine.

JULIA WARD HOWE

CENTENNIAL HYMN

Our fathers' God! from out whose hand
The centuries fall like grains of sand,
We meet today, united, free,
And loyal to our land and Thee,
To thank Thee for the era done,
And trust Thee for the opening one.

Here, where of old, by Thy design,
The fathers spake that word of Thine
Whose echo is the glad refrain
Of rended bolt and falling chain,
To grace our festal time, from all
The zones of earth our guests we call.

Be with us while the New World greets
The Old World thronging all its streets,
Unveiling all the triumphs won
By art or toil beneath the sun;
And unto common good ordain
This rivalship of hand and brain.

Thou, who hast here in concord furled
The war flags of a gathered world,
Beneath our western skies fulfil
The Orient's mission of goodwill,
And, freighted with love's Golden Fleece,
Send back its Argonauts of peace.

For art and labor met in truce,
For beauty made the bride of use,
We thank Thee; but, withal, we crave
The austere virtues strong to save,
The honor proof to place or gold,
The manhood never bought nor sold!

Oh make Thou us, through centuries long,
In peace secure, in justice strong;
Around our gift of freedom draw
The safeguards of Thy righteous law:
And, cast in some diviner mould,
Let the new cycle shame the old!

JOHN GREENLEAF WHITTIER

The New Colossus

Not like the brazen giant of Greek fame,
With conquering limbs astride from land to land;
Here at our sea-washed, sunset gates shall stand
A mighty woman with a torch, whose flame
Is the imprisoned lightning, and her name
Mother of Exiles. From her beacon-hand
Glows worldwide welcome; her mild eyes command
The air-bridged harbor that twin cities frame.

"Keep, ancient lands, your storied pomp!" cries she
With silent lips. "Give me your tired, your poor,
Your huddled masses yearning to breathe free,
The wretched refuse of your teeming shore.
Send these, the homeless, tempest-tost to me,
I lift my lamp beside the golden door!"

EMMA LAZARUS, 1883,
inscribed on the Statue of Liberty, 1903

THE PRESIDENCY

The president of the United States occupies a position of peculiar importance. In the whole world there is probably no other ruler, certainly no other ruler under free institutions, whose power compares with his. Of course a despotic king has even more, but no constitutional monarch has as much.

In the republics of France and Switzerland the president is not a very important officer, at least, compared with the president of the United States. In England the sovereign has much less control in shaping the policy of the nation, the prime minister occupying a position more nearly analogous to that of our president. The prime minister, however, can at any time be thrown out of office by an adverse vote, while the president can only be removed before his term is out for some extraordinary crime or misdemeanor against the nation.

Of course, in the case of each there is the enormous personal factor of the incumbent himself to be considered, entirely apart from the power of the office itself. The power wielded by Andrew Jackson was out of all proportion to that wielded by Buchanan, although in theory each was alike. So a strong president may exert infinitely more influence than a weak prime minister, or vice versa. But this is merely another way of stating that in any office the personal equation is always of vital consequence.

It is customary to speak of the framers of our Constitution as having separated the judicial, the legislative, and the executive functions of the government. The separation, however, is not in all respects sharply defined. The president has certainly most important legislative functions, and the upper branch of the national legislature shares with the president one of the most important of his executive functions; that is, the president can either sign or veto the bills passed by Congress, while, on the other hand, the Senate confirms or rejects his nominations. Of course, the president cannot initiate legislation, although he can recommend it. But unless two-thirds of Congress in both branches are hostile to him, he can stop any measure from becoming a law. This power is varyingly used by different presidents, but it always exists, and must always be reckoned with by Congress. . . .

The immense federal service, including all the postal employees, all the customs employees, all the Indian agents, marshals, district attorneys, navy-yard employees, and so forth, is under the president. It would of course be a physical impossibility for him to appoint all the individuals in the service. His direct power lies over the heads of the departments, bureaus, and more important offices. But he does not appoint these by himself. His is only the nominating power. It rests with the Senate to confirm or reject the nominations.

The senators are the constitutional advisers of the president, for it must be remembered that his Cabinet is not in the least like the Cabinet of which the prime minister is head in the English Parliament. Under our government, the secretaries who form the Cabinet are in the strictest sense the president's own ministerial appointees; the men, chosen out of all the nation, to whom he thinks he can best depute the most important and laborious of his executive duties. . . .

But although many men must share with the president the responsibility for different individual actions, and although Congress must of course also very largely condition his usefulness, yet the fact remains that in his hands is infinitely more power than in the hands of any other man in our country during the time that he holds the office; that there is upon him always a heavy burden of responsibility; and that in certain crises this burden may become so great as to bear down any but the strongest and bravest man. . . .

We have had presidents who have acted very weakly or unwisely in particular crises. We have had presidents the sum of whose work has not been to the advantage of the republic. But we have never had one concerning whose personal integrity there was so much as a shadow of a suspicion, or who has not been animated by an earnest desire to do the best possible work that he could for the people at large. Of course infirmity of purpose or wrong-headedness may mar this integrity and sincerity of intention; but the integrity and the good intentions have always existed. We have never had in the presidential chair any man who did not sincerely desire to benefit the people and whose own personal ambitions were not entirely honorable, although as much cannot be said for certain aspirants for the place, such as Aaron Burr. . . .

In the easiest, quietest, most peaceful times the president is sure to have great tasks before him. The simple question of revenue and expenditure is as important to the nation as it is to the average household, and the president is the man to whom the nation looks and whom it holds accountable in the matter both of expenditure and of revenue. It is an entirely mistaken belief that the expenditure of money is simply due to a taste for recklessness and extravagance on the part of the people's representatives.

The representatives in the long run are sure to try to do what the people effectively want. The trouble is that although each group has, and all the groups taken together still more strongly have, an interest in keeping the expenditures down, each group has also a direct interest in keeping some particular expenditure up. This expenditure is usually entirely proper and desirable, save only that the aggregate of all such expenditures may be so great as to make it impossible for the nation to go into them.

It is a good deal the same thing in the nation as it is in a state. The demand may be for a consumptive hospital, or for pensions to veterans, or for a public building, or for an armory, or for cleaning out a harbor, or for starting irrigation. In each case the demand may be in itself entirely proper, and those interested in it, from whatever motives, may be both sincere and strenuous in their advocacy. But the president has to do on a large scale what every governor of a state has to do on a small scale, that is, balance the demands on the Treasury with the capacities of the Treasury.

Whichever way he decides, some people are sure to think that he has tipped the scale the wrong way, and from their point of view they may conscientiously think it; whereas from his point of view he may know with equal conscientiousness that he has done his best to strike an average which would on the one hand not be niggardly toward worthy objects, and on the other would not lay too heavy a burden of taxation upon the people. . . .

It is only once in a generation that such a crisis as the Spanish War or the Mexican War or the War of 1812 has to be confronted, but in almost every administration lesser crises do arise. They may be in connection with foreign affairs, as was the case with the Chilean trouble under President Harrison's administration, the Venezuelan matter in President Cleveland's second term, or the Boxer uprising in China last year. Much more often they relate to domestic affairs, as in the case of a disastrous panic, which produces terrible social and industrial convulsions. . . .

Perhaps the two most striking things in the presidency are the immense power of the president, in the first place; and in the second place, the fact that as soon as he has ceased being president he goes right back into the body of the people and becomes just like any other American citizen. While he is in office he is one of the half-dozen persons throughout the whole world who have most power to affect the destinies of the world.

He can set fleets and armies in motion; he can do more than any save one or two absolute sovereigns to affect the domestic welfare and happiness of scores of millions of people. . . .

During the president's actual incumbency of his office the tendency is perhaps to exaggerate not only his virtues but his faults. When he goes out he is simply one of the ordinary citizens, and perhaps for a time the importance of the role he has played is not recognized. True perspective is rarely gained until years have gone by.

Altogether, there are few harder tasks than that of filling well and ably the office of president of the United States. The labor is immense, the ceaseless worry and harassing anxiety are beyond description. But if the man at the close of his term is able to feel that he has done his duty well; that he has solved after the best fashion of which they were capable the great problems with which he was confronted, and has kept clean and in good running order the governmental machinery of the mighty republic, he has the satisfaction of feeling that he has performed one of the great world-tasks, and that the mere performance is in itself the greatest of all possible rewards.

New York Governor
Theodore Roosevelt, 1900

Third Inaugural Address of President Franklin Delano Roosevelt

January 20, 1941

On each national day of inauguration since 1789, the people have renewed their sense of dedication to the United States.

In Washington's day the task of the people was to create and weld together a nation.

In Lincoln's day the task of the people was to preserve that nation from disruption from within.

In this day the task of the people is to save that nation and its institutions from disruption from without.

To us there has come a time, in the midst of swift happenings, to pause for a moment and take stock—to recall what our place in history has been, and to rediscover what we are and what we may be. If we do not, we risk the real peril of isolation, the real peril of inaction.

Lives of nations are determined not by the count of years but by the lifetime of the human spirit. The life of a man is three-score years and ten: a little more, a little less. The life of a nation is the fullness of the measure of its will to live.

There are men who doubt this. There are men who believe that democracy, as a form of government and a frame of life, is limited or measured by a kind of mystical and artificial fate—that, for some unexplained reason, tyranny and slavery have become the surging wave of the future—and that freedom is an ebbing tide.

But we Americans know that this is not true.

Eight years ago, when the life of this republic seemed frozen by a fatalistic terror, we proved that this is not true. We were in the midst of shock—but we acted. We acted quickly, boldly, decisively.

These later years have been living years—fruitful years for the people of this democracy. For they have brought to us greater security and, I hope, a better understanding that life's ideals are to be measured in other than material things.

Most vital to our present and to our future is this experience of a democracy which successfully survived crisis at home; put away many evil things; built new structures on enduring lines; and, through it all, maintained the fact of its democracy.

For action has been taken within the three-way framework of the Constitution of the United States. The coordinate branches of the government continue freely to function. The Bill of Rights remains inviolate. The freedom of elections is wholly maintained. Prophets of the downfall of American democracy have seen their dire predictions come to naught.

No, democracy is not dying.

We know it because we have seen it revive—and grow.

We know it cannot die—because it is built on the unhampered initiative of individual men and women joined together in a common enterprise—an enterprise undertaken and carried through by the free expression of a free majority.

We know it because democracy alone, of all forms of government, enlists the full force of men's enlightened will.

We know it because democracy alone has constructed an unlimited civilization capable of infinite progress in the improvement of human life.

We know it because, if we look below the surface, we sense it still spreading on every continent—for it is the most humane, the most advanced, and in the end the most unconquerable of all forms of human society.

A nation, like a person, has a body—a body that must be fed and clothed and housed, invigorated and rested, in a manner that measures up to the standards of our time.

A nation, like a person, has a mind—a mind that must be kept informed and alert, that must know itself, that understands the hopes and the needs of its neighbors—all the other nations that live within the narrowing circle of the world.

A nation, like a person, has something deeper, something more permanent, something larger than the sum of all its parts. It is that something which matters most to its future—which calls forth the most sacred guarding of its present.

It is a thing for which we find it difficult—even impossible—to hit upon a single, simple word.

And yet, we all understand what it is—the spirit—the faith of America. It is the product of centuries. It was born in the multitudes of those who came from many lands—some of high degree, but mostly plain people—who sought here, early and late, to find freedom more freely.

The democratic aspiration is no mere recent phase in human history. It is human history. It permeated the ancient life of early peoples. It blazed anew in the Middle Ages. It was written in Magna Charta.

In the Americas its impact has been irresistible. America has been the New World in all tongues, and to all peoples, not because this continent was a new-found land, but because all those who came here believed they could create upon this continent a new life—a life that should be new in freedom.

Its vitality was written into our own Mayflower Compact, into the Declaration of Independence, into the Constitution of the United States, into the Gettysburg Address.

Those who first came here to carry out the longings of their spirit, and the millions who followed, and the stock that sprang from them—all have moved forward constantly and consistently toward an ideal which in itself has gained stature and clarity with each generation.

The hopes of the republic cannot forever tolerate either undeserved poverty or self-serving wealth.

We know that we still have far to go; that we must more greatly build the security and the opportunity and the knowledge of every citizen, in the measure justified by the resources and the capacity of the land.

But it is not enough to achieve these purposes alone. It is not enough to clothe and feed the body of this nation, to instruct, and inform its mind. For there is also the spirit. And of the three, the greatest is the spirit.

Without the body and the mind, as all men know, the nation could not live.

But if the spirit of America were killed, even though the nation's body and mind, constricted in an alien world, lived on, the America we know would have perished.

That spirit—that faith—speaks to us in our daily lives in ways often unnoticed, because they seem so obvious. It speaks to us here in the capital of the nation. It speaks to us through the processes of governing in the sovereignties of forty-eight states. It speaks to us in our counties, in our cities, in our towns, and in our villages. It speaks to us from the other nations of the hemisphere, and from those across the seas—the enslaved, as well as the free. Sometimes we fail to hear or heed these voices of freedom because to us the privilege of our freedom is such an old, old story.

The destiny of America was proclaimed in words of proph-

ecy spoken by our first president in his first inaugural in 1789—
words almost directed, it would seem, to this year of 1941: "The
preservation of the sacred fire of liberty and the destiny of the
republican model of government are justly considered . . .
deeply, . . . finally, staked on the experiment intrusted to the
hands of the American people."

If you and I in this later day lose that sacred fire—if we let
it be smothered with doubt and fear—then we shall reject the
destiny which Washington strove so valiantly and so trium-
phantly to establish. The preservation of the spirit and faith of
the nation does, and will, furnish the highest justification for
every sacrifice that we may make in the cause of national defense.

In the face of great perils never before encountered, our
strong purpose is to protect and to perpetuate the integrity of
democracy.

For this we muster the spirit of America, and the faith of
America.

We do not retreat. We are not content to stand still. As
Americans, we go forward, in the service of our country, by the
will of God.

PLEDGE OF ALLEGIANCE
TO THE FLAG

I pledge allegiance to the flag of the United States of America and to the republic for which it stands, one nation under God, indivisible, with liberty and justice for all.